PAPER DOLLS
and
PAPER AIRPLANES

Therapeutic Exercises for
Sexually Traumatized Children

By:
Geraldine Crisci, Marilynn Lay & Liana Lowenstein

Illustrations: Dina Steiner
Design and Illustrations: KIDSRIGHTS

KIDSRIGHTS
Charlotte, North Carolina

PAPER DOLLS AND PAPER AIRPLANES

Published by: KIDSRIGHTS
                10100 Park Cedar Drive
                Charlotte, NC 28210
                800/892-5437 or 704/541-0100

10 9 8 7 6 5 4 3
Second Printing

Printed in the United States of America.

ISBN: 1-55864-048-7

CONTENTS

Dedication

To our dear friend and co-author, Marilynn Lay, who passed away shortly after the completion of this book. Marilynn's creativity, courage, and passion for life is an inspiration to us all. She will be greatly missed by family, friends, and the many children whose lives she touched. We hope that through this book, Marilynn's legacy will live on.

PAPER DOLLS AND PAPER AIRPLANES

ACKNOWLEDGMENTS

As in any creative process, many factors contribute to the final product. We would like to take this opportunity to express our gratitude to Jan Hindman whose work has served as a primary inspiration to our own. Through her training and writing, we have been encouraged and enlightened in our clinical work with children and their families. Her leadership and clinical expertise has provided the conceptual framework from which our work has developed.

From idea development to final decision on activity production, many discussions, feedback sessions, and general learning happens through a collegial process. The Crisis Support Group Program at the Metropolitan Toronto Special Committee on Child Abuse in Toronto was one of the main forums through which this work evolved. We would like to thank the Committee staff, group leaders, interns, resource people, and the children and families participating in the program.

Special thanks to Mary Weeks and Christina Melnechuck who took the time to carefully review the manuscript of this book and who provided valuable feedback. We would also like to thank the following people who assisted in the activity feedback process: Elsa Montero, Elaine McLaughlin, Gloria Shookner, and Patti Schabas.

We would also like to thank David Dunlop, our computer whiz; Gregg Tjepkems, our photographer; and Dina Steiner, our illustrator. We greatly appreciate their creative talents and the time they so generously donated.

In order to protect confidentiality, we didn't photograph any treatment program participants. Therefore, we would like to thank the children and parents of friends and co-workers who volunteered to be photographed for this book.

Finally, we would like to thank our families, friends, colleagues and pets for their continuing support, patience, and good humor during the writing and production of this book.

How This Book Came to Be Written

During a session with a rambunctious group of ten-year-olds, a familiar tug-of-war was in progress. The agenda had been carefully planned, and two experienced therapists were valiantly attempting to carry it out. However, the children weren't focusing on the program. Sally was yawning, Amy was groaning, Lisa was rolling her eyes, and Debra was asking to go to the washroom. The most interesting item in the room appeared to be Amanda's paper dolls, which she had smuggled into the session. The therapists suggested that the paper dolls be handed over for safekeeping until the end of the session.

The group leaders then attempted to redirect the girls' attention to the planned program. There was a further disruption when Lisa began to chew vigorously on the Band-Aid wrapped around her sore finger. The group members chorused, "How grossetating!" which sparked Lisa to gnaw the Band-Aid off with her teeth and spit it accurately at the girl beside her.

The group leaders calmly pointed out that if this behavior continued, the ultimate penalty would be imposed—*no snack*! The girls' rebellion subsided, the exercise was completed almost as planned, and the session came thankfully to an end!

After the girls went home, the two exasperated therapists considered how they could keep the children's attention riveted on the program content. They thought about the paper airplanes, comic books, and stickers that the children had brought to the group counseling—items that frequently became a disruption. The therapists spent some time discussing creative and respectful ways to contain the girls' riotous behavior—and then light dawned! Why not let them play?

For the following group session, the leaders brought their own supply of paper dolls and Band-Aids, thanking Amanda and Lisa for the idea. The paper dolls and Band-Aids became the way for these children to express their pain. This time the girls participated enthusiastically. Their wreaths of paper doll families festooned the table.

At the end of the session, each child held out her string of paper dolls.

"This is me and my family. My mom's the one with all the Band-Aids because she hurts the most," Amy said.

"I'm the doll on the left. I'm tearing it off because I had to go to a foster home after I told," Debra said.

Sally held up her whole family of paper dolls. Each one of them was plastered with Band-Aids.

"My dad has all the Band-Aids because he has to go to jail because I told," Lisa said.

"I put all the Band-Aids on me because I didn't deserve to get abused and it's not my fault," Amanda stated.

Since then we have developed a number of games, stories, and craft activities, which are presented in *Paper Dolls and Paper Airplanes*.

How To Use This Book

Paper Dolls and Paper Airplanes is for mental health professionals who work with sexually abused children in individual or group treatment. It is expected that clinicians using this manual will have a solid understanding of the impact of sexual abuse on children, trauma assessment, and the theory of sexual abuse treatment.

This book provides clinicians with activities and ideas that they can integrate into any sexual abuse treatment framework. The authors are not suggesting a complete treatment program, nor do they present guidelines for a program format. Rather, this book is intended as an adjunct to the therapist's existing model.

THEMES AND ACTIVITIES

Themes. Each chapter begins with a brief overview of the treatment issues related to the particular theme. The thematic chapters may be used in any order depending on the treatment plan or program. For example, one therapist may begin with defining sexual abuse, while another may begin with the issue of disclosure. In some instances, a therapist may devote an entire session to self-esteem. Others may include this topic in each session as a brief segment.

Activities. This book includes many activities for each treatment theme so the therapist can select interventions that are relevant to the child's trauma assessment and help fulfill treatment goals. For example, if a child has strong feelings of self-blame, then the therapist may wish to select activities from the chapter on responsibility.

The activities include paper and pencil exercises, therapeutic games, role playing, puppet shows, stories, and music and art activities. Each activity outlines its suitability as to age and modality and provides goals. The activity lists materials that are necessary to complete the activity plus suggestions as to where particular materials may be obtained. Many activities include worksheets that may be reproduced to use with clients. The book includes step-by-step directions for all activities and a discussion section that further clarifies application, process, and treatment issues.

The activities should not be used as isolated interventions. They are intended to be incorporated into the client's larger comprehensive and multidimensional treatment plan. As James asserts, "Trauma may assault the child physically, cognitively, emotionally, and spiritually, and therefore treatment strategies must deal with each of these dimensions." (1989, p. 14). Therefore, a child's treatment plan might involve individual, group, dyadic, and family therapy, as well as a referral to an extra-curricular activity that reinforces the child's interests and abilities.

Keep in mind the following special circumstances in using this book.

VALIDATED CASES ONLY
The activities in this book are suggested for children who have **validated** cases of sexual abuse. Without a verification by a child protection agency, it wouldn't be possible to do a trauma assessment and, therefore, trauma treatment activities related to the verified abuse. These activities are **not recommended** for pre-disclosure cases.

CRIMINAL COURT CASES
If a child is scheduled to be involved in a criminal court case regarding his/her sexual abuse experience, the clinician should carefully consider whether to include the child in a directive group or individual treatment process prior to trial. The authors strongly urge a discussion with the prosecuting attorney prior to involving the child in this kind of treatment program. The concern to be discussed is the contamination of evidence. Materials, reports, and practitioners are subject to subpoena in criminal court cases. Therefore, decisions to include a child in treatment prior to trial must be carefully assessed, and documentation available which outlines the content and process used.

SEXUALIZED BEHAVIOR (IN GROUP)

It is the experience of the authors that children who present sexualized behaviors will be assessed in regard to this behavior. There are two concerns:

In the case of serious, other-directed sexualized behaviors, fellow group members shouldn't be placed at risk

If a child self-identifies as having this problem, the activities regarding "offenders" will be confusing, difficult, and possibly shaming for the child.

Should the behavior be identified after a child is a member of the group, the leaders will need to consider monitoring plans and, depending on the situation, referral to another service.

GENERAL EXPECTATIONS

Overall, activities should be presented as a choice. It is counter-productive to give the message that a child must participate (of course, group readiness and willingness should be processed prior to group entry).

It is also expected that therapists will use discretion in choosing activities for children. In this way, the treatment program is individualized to the needs of the child.

The activities have been designed to appeal to children and to lower the threat level of the treatment process. It is easy for both therapists and children to enjoy the "fun" aspect of the activity and to forget the process and treatment objectives. Therefore, it is important to emphasize once again that the activities are tools to be used to intervene therapeutically with sexually traumatized children.

We are grateful for the opportunity to share our work. We encourage readers to use their own creative talents and we hope this book appeals to the child within. Most importantly, we hope the activities in this book contribute to the healing process of the brave and resilient children who have been our inspiration.

PAPER DOLLS AND PAPER AIRPLANES

Chapter 1
Defining Sexual Abuse

PURPOSE OF THE CHAPTER:
The purpose of this chapter is to provide victims of child sexual abuse with a definition and framework for understanding the nature and impact of sexual abuse. More often than not, children are surrounded by societal myths that invalidate their experience of being victims of sexual abuse. Therefore, it is important to challenge these myths and to clarify the role of victim and perpetrator.

The activities in this chapter are designed to allow children to:
- acquire a clear definition of child sexual abuse and to gain a vocabulary for ongoing work
- learn about societal myths pertaining to child sexual abuse
- begin to become desensitized to the issue of sexual abuse and to facilitate more open communication on the topic.

Additionally, providing a group specific to sexual abuse treatment begins the process of breaking down the dynamics of isolation and secrecy. The fact that all the members of the group have experienced sexual abuse provides a normalizing factor. This opportunity can only be accessed through the group modality. Experience—peer identification with the experience and peer support for that experience—is one of the unique healing processes available through group intervention.

The reader will note that there are no activities in this chapter for preschool-aged children. The authors believe that Jan Hindman's *A Very Touching Book* is the best resource for helping very young children understand the concept of sexual abuse and, therefore, the reader is referred to that book. The reader should also note that the term *secret touching* is used throughout this book for all preschool activities.

Latency—Teen

Paper Airplanes

MODALITY: Group

GOALS: To provide group members with a definition of child sexual abuse; to clarify children's perceptions of abusive situations; to introduce new concepts relating to sexual abuse, such as pornography, masturbation, and grooming; to provide an opportunity to identify potential self-blame belief systems; to facilitate new disclosures resulting from expanded knowledge about sexual abuse

MATERIALS

➤ Paper

➤ Crayons, markers, stickers

➤ "CLUES TO HELP KIDS KNOW THAT A SITUATION M.U.S.T. BE SEXUAL ABUSE" *following*

➤ Flip chart paper or poster board

➤ Scenarios: "WHAT IS SEXUAL ABUSE?" *following*

METHOD

ADVANCE PREPARATION:

The group leader copies "CLUES TO HELP KIDS KNOW THAT A SITUATION M.U.S.T. BE SEXUAL ABUSE" onto flip chart paper or poster board and tapes it to the wall in the room where the group members will be able to see it.

The 14 "WHAT IS SEXUAL ABUSE?" scenarios are each written onto separate pieces of paper and the papers are then folded into paper airplanes. (Note: Other scenarios may be developed that are more pertinent to the children in the group. The purpose is to allow group members to think about the exact components that make for an abusive situation.)

ACTIVITY:

The activity begins by having each group member write a definition of child sexual abuse on a sheet of paper. The members fold the sheets into paper airplanes and decorate them. The planes can be flown into the air and exchanged among group members. For added fun, a landing strip can be marked on the floor with masking tape and the children can take turns attempting to land their planes.

The children unfold their paper airplanes and take turns reading the definitions aloud to the group. The leader then introduces to the group the "CLUES TO HELP KIDS KNOW THAT A SITUATION M.U.S.T. BE SEXUAL ABUSE." The clues are discussed so that the group members have a clear definition of sexual abuse.

Each child selects a paper airplane from the pile that the leader has brought to the group. Children take turns opening the paper airplanes, reading the scenarios aloud, and deciding if the situation is sexual abuse. The "CLUES" prompt taped to the wall can be used as a guide to help children determine if the situation constitutes sexual abuse.

As each scenario is read aloud, group members are polled for their opinions and are encouraged to express feelings of doubt and confusion surrounding ambiguous situations. *The therapist should note that comments of doubt, confusion, and ambiguity are important.* It is often through a discussion of these issues that therapists identify specific belief systems held by particular children that may bind them to a feeling of responsibility. Moving too quickly to explain or correct, prior to an exploration of the doubts raised, can prematurely address cognitive concerns and seal over emotional distress. This activity can provide a format through which children reveal their real concerns regarding self-blame.

DISCUSSION

Children are often stymied initially at the prospect of defining sexual abuse. The group leader can elicit a comprehensive definition by asking questions, such as:

- Does intercourse have to occur for something to be called sexual abuse?
- What if kids are the same age and they really want to touch each other's private parts?

The leader enables the children to understand that sexual abuse includes many different kinds of activities and involves trickery, deceit, coercion, secrecy, and sometimes force. This is an important activity as it teaches terms, gives information about the nature of sexual abuse, and provides an opportunity to check out what may be ambiguous situations from the child's point of view. Further, it addresses the children's right to privacy and the sanctity of their own bodies.

CLUES TO HELP KIDS KNOW THAT A SITUATION
M.U.S.T.
BE SEXUAL ABUSE

Sometimes it is hard for kids to know if a situation is sexual abuse. Below is a list of clues that will help you sort out some of the confusion about what sexual abuse is.

M	=	Makes me
U	=	Uncomfortable
S	=	Secret
T	=	Tricks

A situation **M.U.S.T** be sexual abuse if the person **Makes** you do something that feels **Uncomfortable,** tells you to keep it a **Secret**, or uses **Tricks** (such as lies or bribes) to get you to go along with the sexual abuse.

DIRECTIONS:

Copy the following information onto a flip chart or poster board. Tape it to the wall.

SCENARIOS

What is Sexual Abuse?

- ➤ Your brother walks into your room without knocking and sees you undressed...is that sexual abuse?

- ➤ The man at the candy store tells you how pretty you are every time you go there and touches your arm...is that sexual abuse?

- ➤ You are wrestling with an uncle and his arm keeps brushing across your breasts...is that sexual abuse?

- ➤ You sit on your dad's lap and he hugs you...is that sexual abuse?

- ➤ Your baby-sitter kisses you on the lips when he tucks you into bed...is that sexual abuse?

- ➤ Your brother always walks into the bathroom when you get out of the shower...is that sexual abuse?

- ➤ Your sister's boyfriend tells you that he has a surprise and he invites you to come close so he can whisper in your ear and then he tries to put his hand down your pants...is that sexual abuse?

- ➤ A boy you like kisses you...is that sexual abuse?

- ➤ Your boyfriend touches your breasts...is that sexual abuse?

- ➤ You and your girl friend are babysitting and you go into the parents' room and look at dirty magazines...is that sexual abuse?

- ➤ A girl you don't like puts her arm around you...is that sexual abuse?

- ➤ Your uncle makes you watch him masturbate...is that sexual abuse?

- ➤ A friend of your dad's is walking around the house nude...is that sexual abuse?

- ➤ Your girl friend's mother touches you in a way that makes you feel uncomfortable...is that sexual abuse?

Latency—Preteen
The Sexual Abuse Game

MODALITY: Individual and group

GOALS: To inform and educate children about the nature and impact of sexual abuse and to enable children to begin to self-disclose

MATERIALS

> Colored index cards or poster board (blue, yellow, green colors)

> Spinner (paper plate, popsicle stick and thumbtack can be used)

> Question Cards *following*

METHOD

ADVANCE PREPARATION:
Construct the Sexual Abuse Game by writing questions on index cards. Write FEELING questions on blue cards, TELLING questions on yellow cards, LEARNING questions on green cards (see following questions). To make the spinner, the attached wheel can be cut out and glued onto a paper plate or piece of cardboard. A popsickle stick can be stuck on with a thumbtack to the middle of the plate.

FEELING CARDS=aim at helping the child identify and express feelings associated with the sexual abuse.
TELLING CARDS=invite the child to share personal information related to the abuse (these questions are more general and require a

related to the abuse (these questions are more general and require a relatively low level of personal disclosure).

LEARNING CARDS=help to teach the child more about the issue of child sexual abuse.

ACTIVITY:

The game is as follows:

- Each player takes a turn at spinning the wheel.
- The spinner lands on a space that corresponds to a particular stack of cards.
- If the spinner lands on ***FREE CHOICE***, the player can select from any of the three categories and choose a card from any stack.
- Once a question card is selected, the player can answer the question, pass, or ask the group (or therapist) for help in answering the question.

DISCUSSION

Children respond well to the board game format because it is a familiar play activity. The game generally elicits material for meaningful therapeutic interchange. In the group setting, the therapist can use the children's responses as a point of departure for further group discussion.

This activity also provides leaders an opportunity to observe which areas—"feeling," "telling," or "learning"—are more comfortable for each child. Through this process, leaders can learn which intervention methods might work best for each child (i.e., expressive or verbal, cognitive or emotional).

QUESTION CARDS

FEELINGS CARDS

❖ FEELINGS CARD ❖	❖ FEELINGS CARD ❖
Name 3 feelings kids often have about being sexually abused.	If you were the parent, what would you say to a child who told you she was being sexually abused?
❖ FEELINGS CARD ❖	❖ FEELINGS CARD ❖
Fill in the blank: "Since I told about the abuse I have been feeling _____ _____ "	What would you say to a child who was upset because she was being teased at school by kids who knew about the sexual abuse?
❖ FEELINGS CARD ❖	❖ FEELINGS CARD ❖
When you told about the sexual abuse, what was the one thing you felt most worried about?	Describe how it felt to keep the secret. Did you want to tell someone? Who?
❖ FEELINGS CARD ❖	❖ FEELINGS CARD ❖
Do you think it is OK for a child to love and hate the abuser at the same time?	Fill in the blank: "I feel proud of myself because_____ _____ "
❖ FEELINGS CARD ❖	❖ FEELINGS CARD ❖
What would you say to a child who felt guilty because she did not say "no" to the sexual abuse?	What would you say to a child who pretended that everything was OK when really she was feeling sad inside?

FEELINGS CARDS

❖ **FEELINGS CARD** ❖

How did you feel after you told about the sexual abuse?

❖ **FEELINGS CARD** ❖

What are some of the reasons why kids sometimes blame themselves for the sexual abuse?

❖ **FEELINGS CARD** ❖

Fill in the blank: "When I think about the sexual abuse, one of the things I feel angry about is _____."

❖ **FEELINGS CARD** ❖

What would you say to a child who felt guilty about telling?

❖ **FEELINGS CARD** ❖

What would you say to a child who felt guilty because her mother was crying all the time?

❖ **FEELINGS CARD** ❖

Fill in the blank: "When I told about the sexual abuse, I was scared that _____ _____."

❖ **FEELINGS CARD** ❖

How did you feel the first time you came to this group?

❖ **FEELINGS CARD** ❖

How does your family feel toward the abuser now?

❖ **FEELINGS CARD** ❖

Fill in the blank: "When I think about the sexual abuse, one of the things I feel sad about is _____."

❖ **FEELINGS CARD** ❖

Fill in the blank: "Now that I have told about the sexual abuse, I hope that_____."

TELLING CARDS

❖**TELLING CARD**❖ Name something that has changed since you told about the sexual abuse: _____ _____	❖**TELLING CARD**❖ If you could say one thing to the person who sexually abused you, what would you say?
❖**TELLING CARD**❖ How did your family find out you were being sexually abused?	❖**TELLING CARD**❖ Have you had bad dreams at night since you were sexually abused?
❖**TELLING CARD**❖ What has helped you the most since you told about the sexual abuse?	❖**TELLING CARD**❖ What has been the hardest thing that has happened since you told about the abuse?
❖**TELLING CARD**❖ Do you ever think that the abuse was your fault?	❖**TELLING CARD**❖ Turn to the person on your left and tell her she was brave for having told about the sexual abuse.
❖**TELLING CARD**❖ How long did you keep the abuse a secret?	❖**TELLING CARD**❖ Who has helped you the most since you told about the sexual abuse?

TELLING CARDS

❖ **TELLING CARD** ❖

Sometimes an abuser will give the child special treats so the child will go along with the sexual abuse, or will keep the abuse a secret. Did this happen to you?

❖ **TELLING CARD** ❖

Besides the kids in this group, do you know any other people who have been sexually abused?

❖ **TELLING CARD** ❖

If you had a magic wand and could have three wishes, what would they be?

❖ **TELLING CARD** ❖

If you could change one thing in your family now, what would it be?

❖ **TELLING CARD** ❖

How have your brothers or sisters reacted to finding out you were abused?

❖ **TELLING CARD** ❖

What was one thing your abuser said or did to make you keep the abuse a secret?

❖ **TELLING CARD** ❖

Do you ever wish that you hadn't told about the sexual abuse?

❖ **TELLING CARD** ❖

What do you think should happen to your abuser now?

❖ **TELLING CARD** ❖

What did the abuser say would happen if you told about the abuse?

❖ **TELLING CARD** ❖

How can your family best help you now?

LEARNING CARDS

❖ LEARNING CARD ❖ What does sexual abuse mean?	**❖ LEARNING CARD ❖** What advice would you give to a child who had to go to court to testify?
❖ LEARNING CARD ❖ True or False: You shouldn't tell if you are being abused, because the abuser will get in trouble.	**❖ LEARNING CARD ❖** What should a child do if the abuser goes to visit the child when he is not supposed to?
❖ LEARNING CARD ❖ If your cousin shows you pictures of naked people in a magazine, is that sexual abuse? What should you do about it?	**❖ LEARNING CARD ❖** True or False: Sexual abuse happens mostly to girls and hardly ever to boys.
❖ LEARNING CARD ❖ Can a person who sexually abuses a child stop from doing this?	**❖ LEARNING CARD ❖** Do children ever sexually abuse other children?
❖ LEARNING CARD ❖ True or False: Most children don't know the person who abused them.	**❖ LEARNING CARD ❖** True or False: An adult has a right to touch a child's private parts.

PAPER DOLLS AND PAPER AIRPLANES

LEARNING CARDS

❖LEARNING CARD❖	❖LEARNING CARD❖
Why do you think kids often keep sexual abuse a secret?	True or False: Children should be punished for not being able to stop the abuse from happening.
❖LEARNING CARD❖	❖LEARNING CARD❖
True or False: It is better to forget about the sexual abuse, rather than to talk about it.	Do you think people can tell that you've been sexually abused simply by looking at you?
❖LEARNING CARD❖	❖LEARNING CARD❖
If you are in the park and a man shows you his penis, is that sexual abuse?	True or False: Children usually tell about everything that happened to them during the sexual abuse when they first talk to someone about it.
❖LEARNING CARD❖	❖LEARNING CARD❖
True or False: A child who touches his or her private parts when alone in bed at night is bad.	What should you do if a child tells you she is being sexually abused?
❖LEARNING CARD❖	❖LEARNING CARD❖
What should a child do if she tells her mother she is being sexually abused and her mother doesn't believe her?	Why do you think kids are not to blame for sexual abuse?

SPINNING WHEEL

Copy the wheel below onto a paper plate or piece of cardboard and attach a spinner to the center of the wheel.

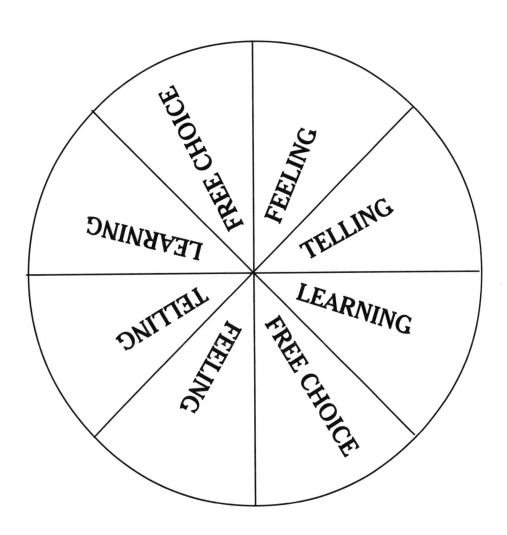

Preteen—Teen
Myths & Facts

MODALITY: Group

GOAL: To challenge commonly held myths about child sexual abuse

MATERIALS

➤   Set of "Myths & Facts" cards *following*

METHOD

ADVANCE PREPARATION:
The therapist cuts out the MYTHS & FACTS cards and glues them onto cardboard squares to form a deck.

ACTIVITY:
The group leader explains that the activity involves playing a card game. The leader fans out the cards and asks for a volunteer to begin the game. The volunteer picks a card from the deck. The volunteer reads the "Myth & Fact" cards which are in the form of questions aloud to the group. The group votes on whether the statement is a myth or fact. The volunteer then reads the answer that is written on the card to the group. Discussion about the statement is encouraged. After the discussion, the volunteer selects another group member to pick the next card and the game continues until all the cards have been used.

DISCUSSION

There are many commonly held beliefs about child sexual abuse which are unfounded. An important part of the victim's rehabilitation process is to challenge the myths and distortions that exist. Education is an essential component of sexual abuse treatment. In this activity, group members learn that:

- Sexual abuse is widespread and they are not alone.

- There are many forms of child sexual abuse.

- Sexual abuse crosses all socioeconomic boundaries.

- Sexual offenders come from all walks of life.

- Children rarely lie about having been abused.

- Sexual abuse does not cause homosexuality.

- Parents often need treatment in order to help their sexually abused children.

It is important for leaders to pursue discussion that includes such questions as:

- Why do some people believe these myths?

- Have you heard people say these things?

- Have you read these myths in newspapers or books?

Teens often know the "right response." If the issues listed here are not raised by the group, it is important for the leader to challenge these myths through the suggested questions. At this age, young people need a framework from which to understand commonly held myths, and to know that the myths can be challenged through correct information. Another approach would be to ask the group members how they think their teachers, classmates, friends, or family members would respond to these myths.

MYTH OR FACT?

Child sexual abuse is rare and happens mostly to girls and hardly ever to boys.

ANSWER: MYTH

According to statistics, 50% of all women and 30% of all men were victims of an unwanted sexual act as children (Badgley, 1984).

MYTH OR FACT?

Sexual abuse happens mostly in poor families.

ANSWER: MYTH

Sexual abuse happens among all groups of the population. It happens in all sociodemographic and education levels.

MYTH OR FACT?

Most sexual abusers are sick and cannot stop themselves from molesting a child.

ANSWER: MYTH

Although the behavior of child molesters is disturbing, most people who sexually abuse a child appear normal, and few have a specific mental illness. Sexual abusers have control over their behavior. They are aware that they are doing something wrong and they are making a choice to abuse a child.

MYTH OR FACT?

Children rarely lie about being sexually abused.

ANSWER: FACT

Children rarely lie about being sexually abused. Even if the abuser is proven not guilty in court, this does not mean that the child was making up the story about being molested.

MYTH OR FACT?

It is easy for victims to stop the sexual abuse from happening. All they have to do is say no.

ANSWER: MYTH

It is very hard for children and adolescents to stop the abuse from happening. Children are taught to obey adults, so it is hard for kids to just say no. Victims are often tricked, bribed, or threatened into going along with the abuse. Abusers are often very tricky and know what to say or do to get kids to go along with the sexual abuse.

MYTH OR FACT?

Victims of sexual abuse sometimes cause the abuse to happen because of how they dress or act.

ANSWER: MYTH

Nothing the victim says or does causes the abuse to happen. It is always the sexual abuser's responsibility, because he or she is making a choice to do something that is wrong.

MYTH OR FACT?

Children are usually sexually abused by a stranger.

ANSWER: MYTH

Most sexual abusers are known to their victims. Sexual abuse victims are most commonly abused by a family member—parent, step-parent, uncle, grandparent, or sibling—or by someone they know and trust like a baby-sitter, teacher, coach, or family friend.

MYTH OR FACT?

Most children who have been sexually abused keep the abuse a secret for a long time.

ANSWER: FACT

It is very common for victims of sexual abuse to keep the abuse a secret because they are afraid of what will happen if people find out, or they worry they won't be believed.

MYTH OR FACT?

Unless sexual intercourse occurs, it's not really sexual abuse.

ANSWER: MYTH

Sexual abuse is when someone uses tricks, secrecy, or force to touch a child's private parts in a way that confuses them, scares them, or hurts them. It is also sexual abuse if someone forces the child to touch him in a sexual way, or takes naked pictures of the child, or makes the child look at pornographic pictures.

MYTH OR FACT?

It is better to forget about the sexual abuse than to talk about it.

ANSWER: MYTH

Although it can be hard to talk about the sexual abuse, it is important for victims to get help and talk about what happened.

MYTH OR FACT?

All boys who are sexually abused by a male are gay.

ANSWER: MYTH

Just because a boy is sexually abused by a male does not mean he is gay. Some boys who are sexually abused may feel confused about their sexual orientation. This is normal and OK. It can help to talk to someone about these confusing feelings.

MYTH OR FACT?

Parents always believe their kids when they tell them they have been sexually abused.

ANSWER: MYTH

Sometimes parents don't believe their kids when they tell them about the sexual abuse, because it's hard for parents to accept that their kids have been hurt or that someone they love has hurt their child. Parents may need time to sort out their feelings and to get the right kind of help in order to be a support to their child.

19

Teen

Survey: 'How Do I Know If I've Been Sexually Abused?'

MODALITY: Individual, group

GOALS: To create a safe and comfortable forum to discuss healthy sexuality, sexual abuse, inappropriate behavior; to validate and affirm the abusive experiences to which victims are subjected; to clarify abusive and potentially high-risk situations

MATERIALS

➤ Survey: "How Do I Know If I've Been Sexually Abused?" *following*

METHOD

ADVANCE PREPARATION:
The group leader makes copies of the survey to be distributed to all group members.

ACTIVITY:
The leader introduces the activity by explaining that sexual abuse is confusing. Some facts and statistics can be given to illustrate that sexual abuse is widespread and misunderstood.

To address the problem of varied reading ability, it is helpful if the leader reads each item aloud to the group. In this way, the leader makes sure that the meaning of each question is clear. After completing the survey, group members discuss their responses with one another.

DISCUSSION

As you carry out this activity, give group members the choice as to whether they will share with the group the nature of the abuse they have experienced. It is extremely important that children feel that their privacy is respected.

This exercise leads naturally into a discussion of sexual issues. The group can examine what constitutes an acceptable sexual relationship. "When is it OK to have sex?" is an individual decision. This exercise offers an opportunity to demonstrate respect for the influences of custom, religion, individual preference, and family beliefs.

Questions which the group can discuss and examine include:

- What is date rape?
- What are the subtle and insidious ways in which victims are made to feel responsible for sexual abuse?

Note: Due to the suggestive or leading nature of this activity, the survey should only be used when the term *sexual abuse* has been defined and substantiated for each group member.

SURVEY

'How Do I Know If I've Been Sexually Abused ?'

HAVE YOU Yes No

1. been made to pose for "sexual" photographs? ☐ ☐

2. been touched on your private parts—your breasts or your genitals—by someone you didn't want to be touched by? ☐ ☐

3. been bathed in a way that made you feel uncomfortable? ☐ ☐

4. been made to touch the genitals of an adult or older kid? ☐ ☐

5. been forced or tricked into watching other kids or adults perform sexual acts? ☐ ☐

6. been in a situation where you felt you couldn't say no to uncomfortable touches, kisses, tickling, or cuddling? ☐ ☐

7. been asked to watch an adult masturbate? ☐ ☐

8. been made to have oral sex? ☐ ☐

9. been forcefully penetrated (having an adult put a finger, penis, or any object inside the vagina or anus)? ☐ ☐

10. been made to have an adult rub up against you in a sexual way? ☐ ☐

HAVE YOU

Yes   No

11. been raped (penetrated using force or threats of violence)? ☐ ☐

12. been subjected to someone exposing their private parts to you (sometimes the abuser acts like it's an accident)? ☐ ☐

13. been told that the clothes you're wearing or the way you're acting are really turning the person on and this should be kept a secret? ☐ ☐

14. been made to watch sex videos or look at pornographic magazines? ☐ ☐

15. been watched while you were in the bathroom or getting dressed? ☐ ☐

Teen
Think Tank

MODALITY: Group

GOALS: To enable teens to begin to discuss issues related to sexual abuse and to assess their knowledge base

MATERIALS

➤ Six pieces of poster board to make question sheets

METHOD

ADVANCE PREPARATION:
The therapists writes one "Think Tank" question on the top of each piece of poster board.

ACTIVITY:
Divide group members into pairs. Provide each pair with one question sheet. Give the pairs 15 minutes to prepare a response to their question. Group members should write responses to the questions underneath the questions on the poster board. Pairs take turns presenting their responses to the rest of the group.

After each pair has completed its presentation, the group can engage in debate. Even if all group members are in agreement with the answers to each question, taking sides and playing the devil's advocate (either with leaders taking opposing views to allow the group to become more cohesive or by dividing members into two groups) allow for possible conflicts or questions to be identified. To allow for a closure process, final resolution should occur for each issue before ending this session of the group.

DISCUSSION

By engaging in a think tank, teens generally feel empowered by developing responses to questions typically asked by sexual abuse victims. This age-group is usually responsive to a brainstorming activity. They also respond well to debate, and the debate format allows leaders the opportunity to check possible areas of confusion. If too many issues are raised through the debate, it is important to write up areas to be resolved in order to provide an externalization of confusing areas. Follow-up can occur during the next group session.

You can use the questions listed below to spark the brainstorming session.

QUESTIONS FOR THE THINK TANK

How would you define sexual abuse?

What are some examples of situations that would be considered sexual abuse?

How come it isn't OK for an adult to be sexually involved with a child?

What are some reasons why victims may keep sexual abuse a secret?

Why do some victims blame themselves for the sexual abuse?

What are some things that victims can do to cope with sexual abuse?

Chapter 2
Family & Community Relationships

PURPOSE OF THE CHAPTER:

Historically, mental health professionals have focused on the child's individual perception of blame as well as the messages given to the child by the offender. An important dimension of this belief system regarding responsibility is often not identified—how the child perceives the family and community response to what has been disclosed. Even in cases where children may seem to understand that they are not to blame for what happened, the family and community response can serve to undermine the healing process. As Hindman (*Just Before Dawn*, 1989) so clearly illustrates in her conceptual framework, belief of responsibility is a multidimensional construct.

The activities in this chapter are divided into two categories:

- Assessment – <u>Paper Dolls</u>, <u>Band-Aids and Blame</u>, <u>Magic Glasses</u>, <u>Me & My Mom</u>, and <u>What Would They Say</u>. The assessment activities are designed primarily to assess the quality of significant relationships and feelings of responsibility as the child perceives them.

- Treatment – The treatment activities are <u>My Helpers</u>, <u>Design a Support Person</u>, and <u>Getting Help</u>. These activities identify who and what is supportive and they generate specific ideas as to how people can help. The treatment activities should be utilized after the assessment activities in this chapter have been completed.

All Ages
Paper Dolls

MODALITY: Individual, group

GOALS: To assess the child's perspective of victimization, responsibility, and family and community support

MATERIALS

- ➤ Paper (preferably legal size)
- ➤ Paper doll outline *following*
- ➤ Clear tape
- ➤ Scissors
- ➤ Pencils, markers
- ➤ Band-Aids (10 per child)
- ➤ Stickers (self-adhesive dots, stars, and happy faces)

METHOD

ADVANCE PREPARATION:
The therapist should become familiar with the process of making paper dolls in order to teach the children how to make them. For younger children, the therapist may have to pre-cut the paper dolls.

To make a string of eight paper dolls:
- Using clear tape, tape both sides of the shorter ends of two sheets of paper together to make one longer piece of paper (letter size paper works best).
- Fold the paper from end to end in half, then fold it in half again, and in half a third time.
- Cut out the pattern of the paper doll (on page 32) and place the pattern on the folded paper so that the end of the hands are touching the side creases of the paper. (Don't worry if the doll outline does not fit exactly.) Trace the doll outline onto the folded paper.
- Cut along the outline of the doll (but do not cut along the creases where the hands touch the ends of the paper).
- Gently pull open the folds and spread out the chain of paper dolls.

For more detailed instruction on how to make paper dolls, see *Let's Make Paper Dolls* by Vivian Huff; Harper & Row Publishers, New York, 1978.

ACTIVITY:
Each child makes a string of eight paper dolls. The therapist instructs the children as follows:

"Label each paper doll by writing the names of the people who are important to you. Include yourself, your family members, and the person who sexually abused you. Be sure to write the names of any other people who are important to you, such as relatives, foster parents, social workers, teachers, close friends, and so on."

Each child is then provided with 10 Band-Aids plus 10 of each of the stickers (dots, stars, and happy faces). The therapist explains:

"Use the stickers to show how you feel about the people in your life. Put Band-Aids on the people who are feeling hurt because of the sexual abuse. You can place all the Band-Aids on one person or you can distribute them among the dolls. You can use all the Band-Aids, none, or just a few. You can place more Band-Aids to show if someone is feeling more hurt. Put dots on the people who you think are to blame for the sexual abuse. Again, you can use as many dots as you like, and you can place them on one person or on several people. Place stars on the people who you think are brave. Use the happy face stickers on the people who know you are not to blame for what happened."

Children can then display their paper dolls to the group and discuss their feelings about the people who are significant to them.

FOR PRESCHOOL CHILDREN:

A simplified version for preschool children can be applied as follows: The child is provided with a string of three pre-cut paper dolls. The therapist labels each doll (one doll to represent the child victim, one doll to represent the abuser, and one doll to represent the child's primary caregiver). The therapist guides the child in using the stickers by saying:

"These Band-Aids are for hurt, like when you feel sad. Put a Band-Aid on the person who you think is feeling hurt or sad because of the secret touching. You can put just one Band-Aid if you think that person is a little bit hurt, or you can put lots of Band-Aids if you think that person is feeling a lot of hurt. If there is anyone else who you think is feeling hurt, you can put Band-Aids on that person too. Now put the dots on the person who is to blame for the secret touching. Explain that blame means whose fault it is, and give an example of blame to ensure the children understand what the concept means. Put the happy faces on anyone who knows you are not to blame for the secret touching. The stars are for bravery. Bravery means doing something that is really hard to do, like swimming in the deep end of the pool for the very first time. Put the stars on the person who is brave."

DISCUSSION

This activity is a valuable assessment tool. Children love stickers and can use them as they wish to illustrate their perceptions of victimization, responsibility, empowerment, and support. According to Hindman (1989) a "healthy" perspective is one in which the child views herself as the victim, the abuser as responsible, and significant others as supportive and believing. If the perspective is skewed, then this information provides the clinician with an important diagnostic tool and forms the basis for the client's ongoing work in treatment.

If desired, other stickers can be used to allow for additional assessment information. For instance, bee stickers can be used to represent "people who are angry" and spider stickers for "people I am afraid of."

Note: This activity should only be used with children once the sexual abuse has been substantiated by child welfare and/or police. As this is an assessment activity, the role of the therapist in this activity is to elicit information from the child by asking open-ended questions, not to tell the child how to feel. For example, if the child places blame stickers on herself, the therapist should not try to correct this by telling the child it was not her fault, but rather, explore with the child why she feels she is responsible for the sexual abuse.

INSTRUCTIONS FOR:
PAPER DOLLS

1) Label each paper doll by writing the names of the people who are important to you. Write a different name on each doll. Include yourself, your parents, and the person who sexually abused you. Be sure to include any other people who are important to you, such as others in your family, relatives, step-parent, foster parent, social worker, therapist, doctor, teacher, police, close friend, etc.

2) Use the stickers to show how you feel about the people in your life:

Band-Aids = The people who are feeling hurt because of the sexual abuse.

Dots = The people who are to blame for what happened.

Stars = The people who are brave because of what happened.

Happy faces = The people who know I am <u>not to blame</u> for the sexual abuse.

Teens
Band-Aids & Blame

MODALITY: Individual, group

GOALS: To assist children in expressing their perceptions of responsibility for the abuse and to evaluate the degree of support as experienced by the child

M A T E R I A L S

➤ Large sheets of paper with a triangle pre-drawn *following*

➤ Packet of 10 Band-Aids for each group member

➤ Sheet of self adhesive dots—20 dots for each member

➤ Stars—at least 20 stars for each member

M E T H O D

ADVANCE PREPARATION:
The therapist copies the triangle onto large sheets of paper.

ACTIVITY:
The children begin the activity by labeling the three corners of their triangle with the names of the victim, the abuser, and the support person. (The support person is the person the child feels is providing the most emotional support. Who the child chooses as the support person is significant assessment information.) The therapist then begins this activity by exploring ways through which we can show that someone is

show?" Similar demonstrations can be used for bravery and for blame. Once the therapist is sure group members understand the concepts, the children apportion the stars, (symbol of bravery) the band-aids (symbols for hurt) and the adhesive dots (symbols of blame) to all three corners of the triangle. The therapist can say, "Place Band-Aids on the people who are hurt, the stars on the people who are brave, and the dots on the people who are to blame. You can place as many stars, dots and Band-Aids as you need to show the hurt, the bravery and the blame."

DISCUSSION

This activity serves as part of an assessment tool by taking into account all three sides of the triangle (the child's perception of responsibility, victimization, and support). The therapist should consider various aspects when interpreting this exercise. For example, even if the child is clear (the offender is responsible), there will still be a self-blame quality if the support system is perceived as excusing the behavior of the offender. The child's ongoing treatment needs are determined by those areas which cloud the issues of the child's complete innocence and the offender's complete responsibility.

This exercise is also helpful in encouraging victims to express a variety of feelings, attitudes, and responses related to sexual abuse. They often spontaneously add other symbols to their triangle. For example, some victims may add "tears" to show who is sorry.

This exercise often leads to members discussing the difference between courage and nerve or risk-taking. Some children award stars to offenders. In processing the activity, these children are able to explain that they think it takes a lot of "nerve" to sexually abuse a little child while the parents are in the next room. This response offers an important opportunity for the therapist to clarify the victim's thinking around risk-taking.

There is an important caution for therapists. While some victims are angry and do feel anger towards an individual who has sexually abused them, others may be ambivalent or confused. Care should be taken to guard against creating a feeling on the part of group members to "please" the therapist by expressing negative feelings towards the offender. A therapist must be sensitive to the ways in which subtle expectations may be conveyed to victims. This can be detrimental and create feelings of shame or rejection.

NOTE: The concept for this activity is directly derived from Hindman's conceptual framework illustrating the "Relationship Perspective" of the trauma assessment tool she developed (Hindman, *Just Before Dawn,* AlexAndria Associates, 1989). (*)

* While the concept for this activity is Hindman's, the activity was developed for the Crisis Support Group Program at the Metropolitan Toronto Special Committee On Child Abuse and is being used with their permission.

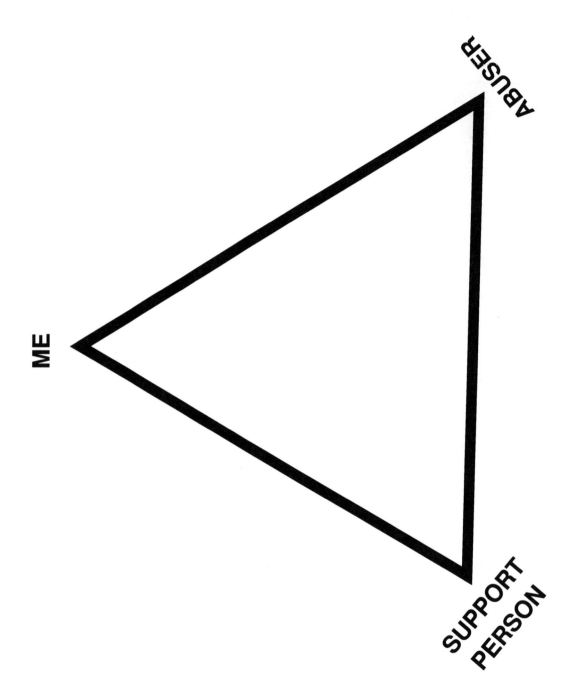

ME

ABUSER

SUPPORT
PERSON

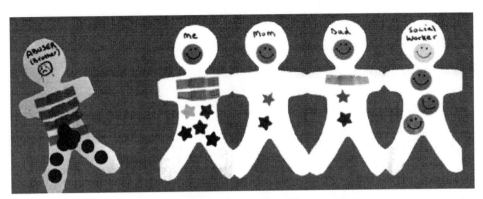

PAPER DOLLS

This string of paper dolls illustrates the child's ambivalence regarding the offender-victim status. In formulating a treatment plan, particular emphasis will be on enabling the child to view the offender as responsible and the child as an innocent victim. It also illustrates the need to enhance the support from the non-offending parent.

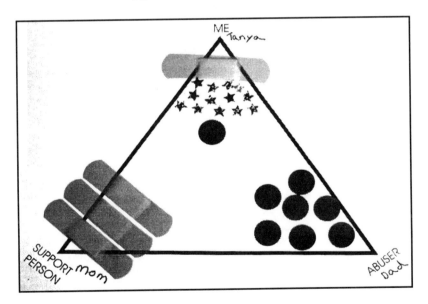

BAND-AIDS & BLAME

The relationship triangle is a powerful assessment tool. This particular configuration portrays the child's conflicted feelings of responsibility and over-concern for the non-offending parent.

All Ages
Me & My Mom

MODALITY: Individual, group

GOALS: To assess parent/child relationships as well as the response to the child's disclosure

MATERIALS

➤ Magazines with a good selection of pictures of women and children

➤ Worksheets: "Me & My Mom" *following*

➤ Scissors, glue sticks

METHOD

ADVANCE PREPARATION:
Copy the "Me & My Mom" worksheets to use with the children.

ACTIVITY:
The therapist provides each child with a set "Me & My Mom" worksheets. The children cut out pictures of women and children from magazines to illustrate their worksheets and to make collages. The second page of the worksheet is a checklist for the children to complete. Children may also cut out the items from the list that apply

to them and incorporate these items into their collages. (Note: Each collage can be put on a separate page if more space is needed.)

If this activity is being used with preschoolers, the therapist should have these children complete one "Me & My Mom" collage rather than a series of collages. The checklist at the end of the chapter should be omitted.

DISCUSSION

This activity is a helpful assessment tool to determine the quality of the victim's relationship with the mother. This area is important to assess because the level of support from the non-offending parent is crucial in determining the victim's healthy resolution to the sexual abuse. The activity will provide the therapist with direction for future dyadic treatment between the victim and the mother.

As a variation of this activity, children can create other collages that assess the various significant relationships in their lives. They may develop collages on such ideas as "Me & My Dad" or "Me & My Foster Parents."

PAPER DOLLS AND PAPER AIRPLANES

WORKSHEET

ME

&

MY

MOM

ME & MY MOM BEFORE THE SEXUAL ABUSE

ME & MY MOM WHEN SHE FOUND OUT ABOUT THE SEXUAL ABUSE

ME & MY MOM NOW

ME & MY MOM...THE WAY I WISH IT WOULD BE

ME& MY MOM CHECKLIST

FROM THE LIST BELOW, CHECK THE ITEMS THAT APPLY TO YOU AND YOUR MOM:

- ☐ My mom tells me the sexual abuse is not my fault.
- ☐ My mom blames me for the sexual abuse.
- ☐ My mom tells me she loves me.
- ☐ My mom ignores me.
- ☐ My mom visits me.
- ☐ My mom talks with me when I am upset.
- ☐ My mom tells me not to talk about the sexual abuse.
- ☐ My mom cries a lot.
- ☐ My mom blames the abuser for what has happened.
- ☐ My mom makes me feel scared.
- ☐ My mom wishes I hadn't told about the sexual abuse.
- ☐ My mom is glad I told about the sexual abuse.
- ☐ My mom believes the abuser.
- ☐ My mom makes sure I have food to eat.
- ☐ My mom makes sure I have clothes to wear.
- ☐ My mom takes care of me when I am sick.
- ☐ My mom reads me bedtime stories.
- ☐ My mom yells at me a lot.
- ☐ I wish I was living with my mom.
- ☐ My mom and I love each other.
- ☐ My mom thinks I am lying about the sexual abuse.
- ☐ I wish my mom would believe me.
- ☐ My mom gives more attention to my brother/sister.

Preschool
My Helpers

MODALITY: Individual, group

GOALS: To strengthen and affirm the victim's sense of support from family and community members

MATERIALS

➤ Picture sheet: "My Helpers" *following*

➤ Situation cards *following*

➤ Scissors

➤ Bag

➤ Crayons

METHOD

ADVANCE PREPARATION:
Cut out the situation cards and place them in a bag.

ACTIVITY:
The group leader introduces the activity by stating that everybody has problems or worries and that many people can help with these problems. Here's an example: "If a kid eats too much ooey gooey chocolate cake and gets a stomachache, who can help that kid to feel better?" Children can volunteer their suggestions and discuss the various adults who can provide help. They will probably mention

parents, step-parents, relatives, foster parents, baby-sitters, doctors, etc. Next, the leader provides each child with a "My Helpers" picture sheet. Children take turns selecting a situation card from the bag and having their care-giver or group leader read it aloud. Then children draw a circle around the person on their picture sheet who can help with the problem identified in the situation card. Children can circle a helper more than once. They can then color their picture sheets.

DISCUSSION

This activity will help young children to identify various family and community supports and to label how different people in their lives can help them. This is particularly important for children who lack support from their families because the activity will help them understand that help and support can come from other adults.

SITUATION CARDS

Who can help me if I'm having a scary dream at night?	Who can help me to cross the street?
Who can help me if someone steals my bike?	Who can help me feel better by cuddling with me?
Who can help me if someone touches me on my private body parts and tells me to keep it a secret?	Who can help me if other kids are being mean to me?
Who can help me if I get stung by a bee?	Who can help me if my big brother/sister hits me?

MY HELPERS

Latency-Teen

Magic Glasses

MODALITY: Individual, group

GOALS: To assess the victim's perspective of level of support for the offender and for self

MATERIALS

➤ Toy sunglasses (preferably in assorted shapes and colors)

➤ Worksheet: "Magic Glasses" *following*

➤ Pencils

➤ Optional: Colored cardboard, red and blue cellophane, glue, scissors

METHOD

ADVANCE PREPARATION:
Collect a number of toy sunglasses and place them on the table in the session room. Copy the worksheet to use with the children.

ACTIVITY:
The children begin by trying on the assortment of glasses. The therapist asks group members to pretend that the glasses are magic and that they allow people to see how someone else views a situation. The therapist then distributes the worksheets to group members. The children complete the worksheets using the glasses as they proceed

through the questions. For younger children, the therapist may need to explain the concept of "different points of view."

As a closing activity, the children can make their own set of 3-D glasses to take home.

Here are the directions:
- Draw an eyeglass pattern onto brightly colored construction paper or cardboard.
- Cut out the pattern.
- Cut out one piece of red cellophane paper and one piece of blue cellophane paper (the pieces should be large enough to cover the eye holes on the glasses).
- Tape or glue the cellophane lenses in place. One lens should be covered with red cellophane and the other with blue cellophane in order to give the 3-D effect.

DISCUSSION

This activity is primarily an assessment tool from which the therapist can develop a treatment plan. The child's perception of himself, the offender, and family relationships can be used as a springboard for further intervention. The children can wear and exchange glasses as they complete the activity. Using the glasses gives the children some emotional distance and adds an element of fun which makes the activity less threatening.

PAPER DOLLS AND PAPER AIRPLANES

WORKSHEET

MAGIC GLASSES

Imagine that you can put on magic glasses that help you see things the way others do. In the situations below, describe them from your point of view, then through the other person's eyes.

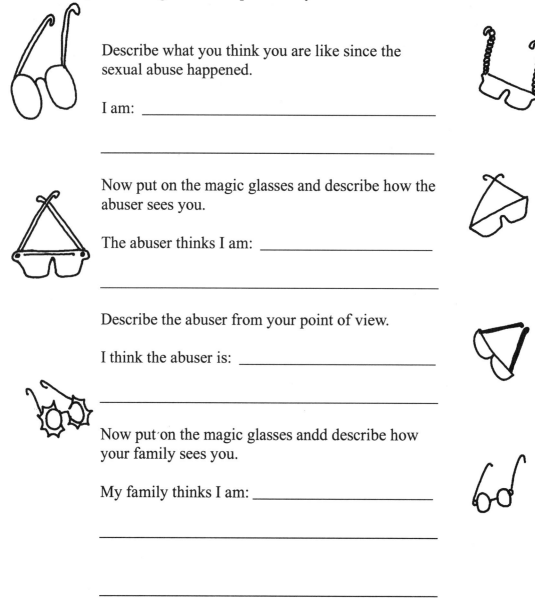

Describe what you think you are like since the sexual abuse happened.

I am: _____

_____

Now put on the magic glasses and describe how the abuser sees you.

The abuser thinks I am: _____

_____

Describe the abuser from your point of view.

I think the abuser is: _____

_____

Now put on the magic glasses andd describe how your family sees you.

My family thinks I am: _____

_____

_____

Describe your family from your point of view.

I think my family is: _____

_____

Now put on the magic glasses and describe how your family see you.

My family thinks I am: _____

_____

Put on another pair of glasses and describe how your family sees the abuser.

My family thinks the abuser is: _____

_____

Put on another pair of glasses and describe how the abuser's family sees him/her.

The abuser's family think the abuser is: _____

_____

_____

Put on another pair of glasses and describe how your friends see you.

My friends think I _____

_____

_____

Latency-Teen
What Would They Say?

MODALITY: Individual, group

GOALS: To assess the victim's feelings toward the offender; to assess the victim's perception of level of support for the offender; to assess the victim's relationship with family and significant others.

MATERIALS

➤ Worksheet: "What Would They Say?" *following*

➤ Blank message bubbles

➤ Pre-prepared message bubbles

➤ Scissors

➤ Glue

➤ Pens/pencils

METHOD

ADVANCE PREPARATION:
Copy the worksheet and blank message bubbles to distribute to the children.

ACTIVITY:

The first part of this activity consists of identifying the significant people in the child's life. It also identifies who knows about the sexual abuse besides the victim and the offender.

The group leader can assist the children by prompting them for information. The leader may say, "Let's start by naming the people who are important to you." The names of these people are listed as the children mention them.

The same process is used for the other categories. The section labeled *Community* would include police, child protection workers, religious leaders, group leaders, teachers, etc.

When group members have identified names for each category, they can be given blank cartoon bubbles to express messages that they feel are being sent to or by the offender. Make sure there are plenty of blank bubbles so the children can share their own ideas and perceptions and not feel restricted. Next, give the children the pre-prepared message bubbles and they can add to their worksheets those messages that apply to their situation.

DISCUSSION

An important issue in the healing for childhood sexual abuse victims is the clarification of the victim-offender relationship. Children who view themselves as innocent victims and view the offender as responsible for the sexual abuse are less likely to be severely traumatized.

This exercise allows children to express the messages that they perceive. Messages such as, "He didn't mean to," "He just got carried away," "Poor guy" will need an intervention plan designed to address this perception. This plan will help the victim alter perceptions and cognitive distortions.

WORKSHEET

PUT WORDS IN THEIR MOUTH— WHAT WOULD THEY SAY?

Community

Abuser's Family and Friends

Abuser

Your Family and Friends

You

WHAT WOULD THEY SAY MESSAGE BUBBLES

Poor Guy!			Don't you want him to come home?
He's sick.			He was drunk.
I believe him.			He didn't mean to.
He just got carried away.			His wife was cold.
I'll hurt you!		I'll hurt someone you love!	

WHAT WOULD THEY SAY MESSAGE BUBBLES

I'm sorry.			I forced you.
I'm a sex offender.			I was drunk.
If she says I did it, then I did it.			I really love you.
She's lying!			It's my fault.

WHAT WOULD THEY SAY MESSAGE BUBBLES

Hooray for you!	I'm glad you told!	It's not your fault.	You're brave!
It took guts to tell.	Now you're safe.	Other kids won't get abused.	Now he can get help.
It happens to lots of kids!	All your feelings are ok.	We all need help.	You're ok!
He knew what he did.	I'll protect you.	How could I have let this happen?	What happened to you was a crime.

Latency-Teen
Design a Support Person

MODALITY: Individual, group

GOALS: To identify the kind of support which the child perceives as helpful; to assess the level of support family and community members are presently providing to the child

MATERIALS

➤ Worksheet: "Design a Support Person" *following*

➤ Crayons, colored pencils, markers

➤ Flip chart and markers

➤ Scissors

➤ Glue

➤ Glitter, scraps of cloth, wrapping paper etc.

➤ Pens

METHOD

ADVANCE PREPARATION:
The therapist makes copies of the worksheet and assembles the materials.

ACTIVITY:

The therapist begins this activity with a discussion of support. Children will contribute their ideas of what they would like someone to say and what they would like someone to do with them and for them. Group members can brainstorm ideas as the therapist records the suggestions on a chalkboard or a flip chart.

The second part of the activity consists of having group members complete the worksheet for their ideal support person. Then children can color and decorate the worksheets.

Children can branch out to design advertisements, posters, etc. Then these can be shared with other group members.

DISCUSSION

This activity is a non-threatening approach for children to express their needs and expectations of others. The therapist can skillfully guide the discussion to help children gain skills in asking for support and acknowledging existing support and resources. The activity can be used to build group cohesiveness as support persons include group members and leaders.

As in "My Helpers" activity in this chapter, the therapist should note that some children will have difficulty in identifying support persons. In this case, the therapist may need to help the children make a list of support people before the children attempt to complete this activity.

WORKSHEET

DESIGN A SUPPORT PERSON

Fill in all the qualities that you would like your ideal support person to show. Include things you would like them to say and do as well as how you wish they would feel.

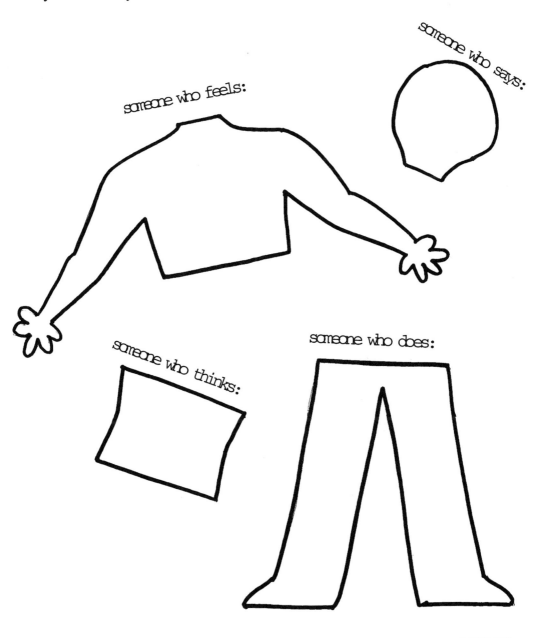

Latency-Teen
Special Flower

MODALITY: Individual, group

GOALS: To affirm the child's existing support system; to recognize the child's own strengths and abilities

MATERIALS

➤ Worksheet: Special Flower *following*

➤ Help Sheet *following*

➤ Salt

➤ Colored chalk

➤ Clear plastic cups or clear glass bottles, such as baby food jars

➤ White glue

➤ Artificial flowers

➤ Glitter

METHOD

ADVANCE PREPARATION:
The therapist copies the worksheet and the help sheet to distribute to group members. Materials as listed need to be collected to use in this activity.

ACTIVITY:

The therapist introduces the activity by leading a discussion on what plants need to thrive and flower.

The first part of the activity involves the completion of the "Special Flower" worksheet. Children can use the help sheet to assist them in completing the worksheet. Next, group members complete an art activity to symbolize the support they get and how their supporters have nurtured their growth. To demonstrate the art activity, the leader shows how chalk can be rubbed over a small quantity of salt to change its color.

Each group member is provided with a glass jar (or plastic cup), salt, and an assortment of colored chalk. Group members decide which color chalk represents each of their supports; e.g., mom=pink, teacher=green, etc. Group members fill their jars with the colored chalk/salt mixture, using the different colors to represent their various support people. A flower is planted in the salt. Glue is poured over the top to seal the mixture and glitter is sprinkled on for decoration.

DISCUSSION

Children who have been sexually abused often feel a sense of isolation. This activity will enable victims to express concretely the support they currently have. The activity acts as a metaphor for how their support persons help them to survive and grow. Some children do not have obvious support persons functioning in their lives and the therapist may need to explore alternatives prior to the children's attempts to complete the exercise.

WORKSHEET

A SPECIAL FLOWER

Fill in the flower pot by writing the support you have (the people who help you, how they help you, and your own strengths and resources). You can use the attached help sheet to make this list. Color in the flower to reflect how these supports have nurtured your growth into a special flower!

HELP SHEET

A SPECIAL FLOWER

MY HELPERS

- Family members
- Relatives
- Foster parents
- Teacher
- Social worker
- Therapist
- Therapy group
- Crisis phone line
- Friend
- Religious leader
- Doctor
- Coach
- Lawyer
- Police officer
- Pet
- Other:_____

MY OWN STRENGTHS AND RESOURCES

- Ability to ask for help
- Ability to talk about my problems
- Ability to stand up for myself
- Eating healthy
- Exercising
- Restful sleep
- Doing things that give me pleasure
- Learning new things
- Trying my best
- Laughing
- Kindness
- Bravery
- Good decision making
- Friendliness
- Accepting myself
- Other:_____

HOW PEOPLE CAN HELP ME

- Believe me
- Be patient with me
- Take care of me when I am sick
- Listen to me
- Have fun with me
- Call me
- Offer advice
- Help me with my schoolwork
- Keep me safe

- Tell me I'm not to blame
- Stand up for me
- Teach me
- Comfort me
- Visit me
- Hug me
- Other:_____

Preteen – Teen
Getting Help

MODALITY: Group

GOALS: To identify existing supports; to develop and strengthen formal and informal support systems; to promote the concepts of seeking appropriate help for worries and concerns

MATERIALS

➤ Pens

➤ Markers/crayons

➤ Set of "TROUBLE CARDS" *following*

➤ 8 to 10 Manila envelopes or brown paper bags

➤ Box of small envelopes

➤ Index cards

METHOD

ADVANCE PREPARATION:
Various trouble card situations are copied onto index cards. The therapist can use discretion as to the number and type of situations. Include a mix of major and minor problems dealing with both general childhood worries and specific concerns about sexual abuse.

ACTIVITY:
The therapist introduces this activity by asking the group for a list of

people who can help kids with problems. Each suggestion is written on a brown paper bag (helper envelopes).

Next, group members choose cards from the stack of "TROUBLE CARDS" and take turns reading situations to the group. Group members discuss possible ways to get help for each situation and take the "TROUBLE" to a "HELPER." This is done by putting the card in the appropriate "HELPER" envelope.

The last part of the activity consists of each group member identifying personal concerns or worries and writing individual "TROUBLE CARDS." Each member shares his or her concerns with the group and states in which "HELPER" envelope each "TROUBLE CARD" will be placed.

DISCUSSION

Because children who have been sexually abused often feel isolated, they frequently need to be taught that problems can be openly talked about. Victims also need to know there are adults (both professional and non-professional) who are interested in them and who are prepared to assist them with their worries.

This activity can assess how likely a child is to turn to appropriate people and resources for support. It also provides an opportunity for the therapist to encourage and strengthen natural and formalized support systems.

Many children don't know the name of their child protection worker and lack the skills to seek assistance.

The therapist can strengthen "asking for help" skills and teach step-by-step how to get help through role-playing, coaching, and behavioral rehearsal. Children can practice writing letters, calling information services, and making a personal directory of helpers.

This follow-up activity will empower children and increase their self-confidence.

This exercise can also be integrated into the chapter dealing with feelings. Children can use their "asking for help" skills to deal with the problems and stresses identified in *Coping With Feelings*.

TROUBLE CARD SITUATIONS

- You break your word and feel bad.
- You feel guilty all the time.
- You can't talk to your social worker because he's a man.
- You have a toothache but you're afraid of going to the dentist.
- Your teacher makes you feel uncomfortable when she puts her arm around you.
- You don't want to come to this group.
- You're alone for the weekend and feel like hurting yourself.
- You're worried about what might happen to the offender.
- You're losing a lot of weight.
- You're tired all the time.
- You're worried you have a disease.
- You're afraid of the dark.
- You can't concentrate in school.
- You're failing math.
- You're being bullied at school.
- You're worried that your breasts are different sizes. You think it might be because you were sexually abused.
- You're planning a party for your friend, but you are afraid that some kids will bring drugs.
- You're afraid to go to court.
- You're worried you might be abused again.
- You're feeling like nobody understands you.
- You're afraid that someone in your family might hurt the offender.
- Kids at school know about the abuse, and you don't want them to spread it.
- You're afraid that your family will break up.
- You have a friend who tells you he is being sexually abused.
- You're fighting with your brother or sister too much.

Chapter 3
Identifying Feelings

PURPOSE OF THE CHAPTER:
The identification of feelings is the key to all aspects of healthy functioning. Putting feelings into words, understanding the range of feelings people can experience, and expressing feelings all serve as tools in need identification, help-seeking, help-giving, communication, relationship building, and self-care.

Early research into the primary prevention of psychopathology demonstrated that social isolation and lack of creative problem-solving skills were two central factors contributing to psychological dysfunction (Spivak and Schurr, 1974). Feeling identification is the key element in the development of skills preventing social isolation. Coping with feelings (Chapter 4) provides another critical building block in learning to give and receive support.

The activities in this chapter are provided as tools to assist children in the process of feelings identification. While several of the activities are developed within the context of the sexual abuse experience, the basic learning objectives have a broader application.

Preschool
Where I Hurt

MODALITY: Individual, group

GOAL: To enable children to express feelings of hurt, shame, and abandonment associated with sexual abuse

MATERIALS

➤ Large pieces of mural or butcher's paper

➤ Felt-tip Markers

➤ Paints, crayons

➤ Band-Aids

➤ Happy face stickers

METHOD

ADVANCE PREPARATION:
Have several child-sized bodies traced and pre-cut in case some children are uncomfortable with the idea of being touched as their bodies are being traced.

ACTIVITY:
In this activity, the group leader traces around each child to make a full body drawing. The therapist asks each child whether they want their own body drawn or want to choose a pre-cut shape to represent them.

After all group members have their full body drawing, they can be encouraged to decorate their drawings and add body features and clothing. The group leader and care givers can ask the children to name and locate correct body parts.

The next part of the activity involves a discussion of how sexual abuse (secret touching) hurts kids. For example, children can show that their eyes might be hurt because they had to see things during the abuse. Children can then place happy face stickers where they feel happy. (This is done to neutralize and balance negative and positive experiences.)

The final part of the activity consists of giving the children an unlimited supply of Band-Aids. The children are told to place the Band-Aids on their body drawings wherever they were hurt by the secret touching or by having to keep the secret.

Children then share their hurt with other group members if they so choose.

DISCUSSION

Caution must be taken to respect the children's boundaries. They should be encouraged to say no if they find the activity uncomfortable. In addition, they should be encouraged to choose whom they prefer to do the tracing (care giver, leader, or another group member). This choice is an important intervention as it teaches and reinforces the children's right to their own bodies and respects their choices. If a peer is chosen to trace a child's body, the activity should be closely supervised. It is an excellent opportunity to intervene **therapeutically** to coach children on appropriate touching.

Preschool—Latency
Feeling Faces

MODALITY: Group

GOAL: To help group members differentiate between different feeling states and to begin to talk about feelings associated with the sexual abuse

MATERIALS

➤ "Feeling Faces" *following*

➤ Cardboard or poster board

➤ Worksheet: "Feeling Faces" *following*

METHOD

ADVANCE PREPARATION:
The "Feeling Faces" sheets are photocopied so that there are several copies for each group member and two copies to be used for the memory game. Paste two "Feeling Faces" sheets onto cardboard. Cut out each face so that each face is on a separate piece of square cardboard. You should now have two matching faces for each feeling on separate cardboard squares. The squares should all be the same size. The "Feeling Faces" cards are then mixed up in a random order so that pairs are not placed together.

ACTIVITY:

To play the memory game, the "Feeling Faces" cards are laid faces down in four rows of eight cards.

Players take turns turning over any two cards. If the two cards don't match, then they are turned back over. If the player makes a match, the player removes the cards and places them at the side.

When a player matches two "Feeling Faces," that player must tell about a time he or she felt that way. For example, if a player selects two cards that both say "angry," that player must describe a time when he or she felt angry. The player who matches the most pairs wins.

Note: The therapist will need to provide definitions for some of the feelings, because younger children will not know the meaning of these words. The therapist provides a definition and then asks the child to tell about a time when that feeling was experienced. For example, "Guilty is when something is your fault because you did something you were not supposed to do. Can you think of a time you did something you weren't supposed to do and you knew it was your fault?"

The second part of the activity consists of completing the "Feeling Faces" worksheet. Children can use their "Feeling Faces" sheet to cut out the desired feeling faces and glue them onto the corresponding squares on the worksheet. Note that there is ample room in the squares for children to glue more than one "Feeling Face." The therapist may wish to highlight the fact that people often experience more than one feeling at a time. If this activity is being used with preschoolers, then the adult care givers can read the worksheets to the children and the children can glue on the faces.

DISCUSSION

This activity provides young children with a vocabulary to verbalize their feelings. Because both comfortable and uncomfortable feelings are included in the memory game, the activity prepares children to deal with a variety of feelings related to the sexual abuse, such as sadness, anger, and guilt.

In processing this activity, the group leader explains that everyone has feelings, and that it is natural to have all kinds of different feelings—both comfortable and uncomfortable. For younger children who may not understand what some of the feelings mean, the leader can offer an example: "Jealous is when you wish you have something that you don't, like if it's your sister's birthday and she gets a present, you may feel jealous that she gets a present and you don't."

The therapist should also understand that developmentally, young children have difficulty comprehending the concept of ambivalent feelings. It can be helpful for the therapist to say, "Sometimes people have positive and negative feelings at the same time, like I may feel angry at my dog for pooping on the carpet but I also still love him!"

FEELING FACES

Happy	Sad	Mad	Excited
Hopeful	Sorry	Guilty	Brave
Shy	Embarrassed	Jealous	Surprised
Confused	Scared	Loved	Hurt

WORKSHEET

FEELING FACES

Kids who have been sexually abused often have lots of mixed-up feelings inside. For each situation below, show how you feel by drawing a picture or by cutting out faces from the "Feeling Faces" picture sheet. Since people may experience more than one feeling at the same time, you can use more than one picture for each situation.

```
When I was sexually abused, I felt:
```

```
Whenever I thought about telling, I felt:
```

```
On the day that I told, I felt:
```

Whenever I think about the abuse, I feel:

People who know what happened to me feel:

When I _____, I feel:

Preschool-Latency

Ali's Story

MODALITY: Individual, group

GOAL: To enable children to identify a wide range of feelings associated with the sexual abuse

MATERIALS

➤ Story: "Ali and Her Mixed-Up Feeling Balloon"

➤ Balloons

➤ Worksheet: "My Feeling Balloon" *following*

➤ Crayons, markers, or pastels (wide assortment of colors)

METHOD

ADVANCE PREPARATION:
The therapist makes copies of the balloon worksheet for all group members and provides coloring tools.

ACTIVITY:
The therapist reads aloud the story "Ali and Her Mixed-Up Feeling Balloon" to the children. Each child is then provided with a "My Feeling Balloon" worksheet. Children color the balloon by using a separate color crayon to represent each feeling. Children can use more of one color to illustrate feelings that are more intense. Children should make a grid to show which color represents each feeling.

The group leader can use a variety of closing activities that involve balloons. Here are two suggestions:

1) **Balloon messages:** Each child is provided with a balloon (not blown up), a small piece of paper, and a pencil. Children write a balloon message on the piece of paper (they can selest one from the list that follows or make up their own). The paper is then folded and inserted into the balloon. They blow up their balloons with the messages inside. The balloons are randomly exchanged among group members. The children take turns popping their balloons and reading aloud the messages.

2) **Balloon faces:** Each child is provided with a round balloon (blown up) and a marker. Children draw faces on the balloons, with any desired facial expression. The balloons are then exchanged among group members. Children take turns identifying the feelings that are expressed on the faces drawn on the balloons, and they are to tell about a time when they experienced that feeling.

DISCUSSION

Ali's story can be used to help children explore and discuss aspects related to their sexual victimization. Children can identify with Ali, and they can share in her experiences vicariously. Children's sense of isolation about the sexual abuse may be reduced as they realize that other children, even if they are only fictional characters, have been through similar circumstances.

The balloon is used as a metaphor to allow children to conceptualize how their mixed-up emotions can intensify to the point of feeling that they might explode if the feelings are not dealt with.

ALI AND HER MIXED UP FEELING BALLOON

Ali is a young girl, much like each of you sitting here in this group. She has a lot of mixed-up feelings inside her. She has been sexually abused.

Ali kept the secret about being sexually abused for a long time, because she **worried** about what would happen if she told. She thought that people wouldn't believe her and that she would get in trouble.

But after a while, Ali felt that she couldn't keep the secret any longer. So she told her best friend, Harriette, about what was happening. Well, when Harriette learned of Ali's secret, she didn't know what to do. So Harriette suggested that Ali tell the teacher.

Well, you can imagine how **nervous** Ali felt when she told her teacher. She had a funny feeling in her stomach, and she couldn't stop fidgeting. Ali felt even worse when the teacher said that the principal would have to be told. Ali could feel her face get redder and redder as the principal asked her all kinds of questions about exactly what happened. Then the police and a social worker came and asked her even more questions. Ali felt **frustrated** having to repeat the same story over and over again, and she felt **embarrassed** having to talk about such private things with complete strangers.

Then the principal called her mother, and when her mother found out, she began to cry. This made Ali feel **guilty** because she thought it was all her fault for making her mother so upset.

The next day at school, Ali was **horrified** to learn that Harriette had told the other kids about what happened. The kids made fun of Ali, and wouldn't let her join in when they played at recess. Ali hated the kids for teasing her and she was very **mad** at Harriette for telling everyone her secret. Ali felt she had no friends. She was **sad** and **lonely**.

Things at home were different too. Everyone always seemed upset. This made Ali feel **guilty** because she thought it was all her fault.

Ali got depressed because her feelings were so mixed up: **mad**, **sad**, **embarrassed**, **lonely**, all these mixed-up feelings jumbled up inside her. Ali didn't know what to do with all these mixed-up feelings. So she pretended that she had a big balloon inside her stomach where she could keep all her mixed-up feelings. It wasn't a real balloon of course, but Ali pretended to keep all her mixed-up feelings inside this balloon.

Because of all the mixed-up feelings inside her, Ali sometimes did things she never used to do, like getting mad at people for no reason. She threw toys around her room, and yelled and screamed, even at her cat, Whiskers! Often, she had **scary** dreams that would wake her up in the middle of the night. When this happened, she would squeeze her teddy bear really hard and bury her head in the pillow until she fell back to sleep.

Ali felt **relieved** that the abuse had stopped, but she missed how she would be treated as someone special. The person who abused her would buy her candy and would tell her how pretty she was. And when she thought back to the sexual abuse, the thing that really **confused** her was that sometimes when he touched her it felt **good**, and other times it felt **yucky**. Ali felt so **confused**, more mixed-up feelings for her to stuff into the balloon inside her stomach.

Ali didn't know how to feel toward the person who abused her. Sometimes she felt **angry** at him, and other times she still **loved** him. And Ali wondered how her mother felt towards him. Was her mother angry at him for what he did? Did she still love him? Did she feel all mixed-up inside just like Ali? And Ali wondered how her mother felt toward her—did her mother still love her?

One night, while Ali's mother was putting her to bed, her mother said: "Ali, you may not think that people **love** you, but they do, and what happened was not your fault. You are just a little girl, my little girl, and he was the big adult who should have known better. I am **proud** of you for telling. You were very **brave**!" Ali sat there with a big smile on her face. For the first time in a long time, Ali felt **happy**. That night, Ali had a good dream and slept well.

The next week, Ali joined a group where she met other kids who had been sexually abused. Ali felt **surprised** when she met the kids in the group, because she had thought she was the only one in the whole world that this had happened to.

Ali found it helpful to talk to the other kids in the group about her mixed-up feelings. She even told them about the pretend balloon inside her stomach. As Ali began to talk more and more about her feelings, guess what happened? The balloon inside her stomach got smaller and smaller and smaller and smaller and eventually disappeared!

The end!

WORKSHEET

MY FEELING BALLOON

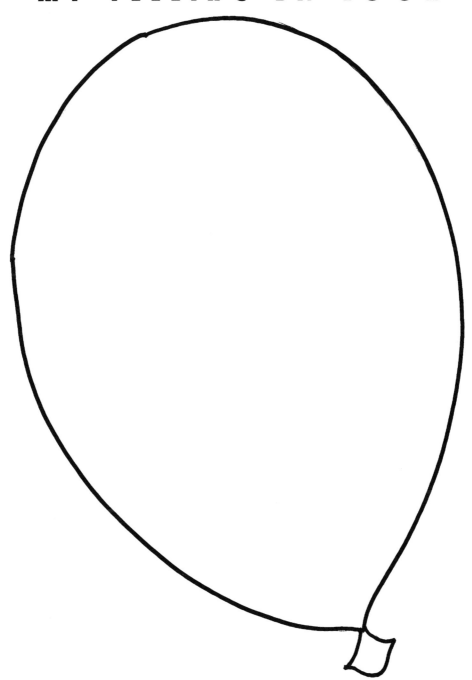

BALLOON MESSAGES

When I am feeling mad, I can punch my pillow.

When I am feeling sad, I can cry.

When I am feeling lonely, I can hug my teddy bear.

When I am feeling confused, I can ask questions.

When I am feeling mad, I can count to ten.

When I am feeling lonely, I can play with my pet.

When I am feeling scared, I can talk to an adult.

When I am feeling lonely, I can ask someone for a hug.

Preschool — Latency
Feelings Mish-Mosh

MODALITY: Individual, group

GOAL: To help children to identify and normalize their various feelings related to the sexual abuse and to encourage the open expression of feelings

MATERIALS

➤ Plastic sandwich bag

➤ 1/2 cup water

➤ Food coloring (an assortment of colors)

➤ Cup

➤ Finger paints and paper

METHOD

ADVANCE PREPARATION:
The therapist collects the finger paints and paper and sets them aside for the children to use for the secons part of this activity. Make sure to label the finger paints (red = mad, blue = sad, yellow = happy, green = scared).

ACTIVITY:
The therapist introduces this activity by stating, "Children usually

have lots of feelings after they have been sexually abused, like sad, mad, or confused." The therapist asks the children to name other feelings that sexually abused children may have. The therapist then affirms that it is normal and OK to have these feelings, and that these children may feel confused or mixed-up inside.

Children are told that they are going to make a "Mish-Mosh of Mixed-Up Feelings." The therapist opens the plastic bag and pours about a half cup of water inside. The therapist then shows the children several colors of food coloring and explains that each color represents a different feeling.

The therapist begins with the blue food coloring. As several drops of the blue food coloring are put in the plastic bag, the therapist says, "Let's pretend this blue food coloring is for the sad feelings we have inside. What are some reasons why kids who have been sexually abused might feel sad?" Children are given an opportunity to respond. The therapist does the same for the other colors (for example, yellow is for happy, red is for mad, and green is for scared).

After several drops of each color have been added to the bag, the therapist seals the bag. The therapist should be careful at this point not to shake the bag, allowing the mixture to maintain its "rainbow" appearance.

The therapist then states, "These colors show all the different feelings we have. If we shake the bag, the feelings get all mixed-up and look kind of yucky. (The therapist shakes the bag.) When we have lots of different feelings, it can be very confusing and we might feel all mixed-up. That's why it's important to talk about the mixed-up feelings so we can let the feelings out and start to feel better." The therapist then opens the bag and pours the liquid out into a sink or a cup, thus metaphorically letting out the feelings. Today we are going to start to talk about our feelings, so we can begin to feel better."

The therapist provides the children with finger paints and a large piece of paper. The finger paints should be labeled with the different feelings (red=mad, blue=sad, yellow=happy, green=scared). Children use the finger paints to make a picture of how they feel about the sexual abuse.

DISCUSSION

The Mish-Mosh Bag is fun to make and excites and fascinates young children. It can be used as an innovative tool to illustrate the concept of mixed-up feelings. The finger painting is then used as a tool to help the children identify and express their feelings. Because this activity is both visual and tactile, it will captivate the children and will help them to learn about and express their feelings.

Latency–Teen

Opinion Poll

MODALITY: Individual, group

GOAL: To assess the victim's perception of responsibility for the sexual abuse, available support, and level of self-esteem

MATERIALS

➤ Flip chart or chalkboard

➤ Paper, markers

➤ Opinion poll *following*

METHOD

ADVANCE PREPARATION:
The therapist makes sure a flip chart or chalkboard and markers or chalkboard and crayons to write with are available. Group members should also be provided with paper and markers. Make copies of the Opinion Poll for group members.

ACTIVITY:
The therapist writes the following statement on a flip chart: "I'm glad I'm here" and asks everyone to draw a circle on a piece of paper. The therapist asks the group members to decide if they agree with the statement, but to keep their responses a secret. The therapist emphasizes that everyone feels different about being in group. Some

kids don't want to be here at all, some kids want to be here a little, and others love to be here. The therapist demonstrates how a person can show thoughts and feelings about things by coloring in portions of a circle.

I'm glad I'm here!

| TOTALLY TRUE | A LITTLE TRUE | NOT AT ALL TRUE |

For the next part of the activity, the therapist distributes the opinion poll and reads through the items with the group. The group members color in the circles to illustrate how they feel about each item on the opinion poll.

DISCUSSION

This activity gives a comprehensive assessment of the child's perception of responsibility, emotional support, and self-concept. The therapist is able to gain a more accurate snapshot of the children's thoughts and feelings when they color in the circles to represent how strong their individual feelings are about specific issues.

OPINION POLL

Fill in the circles to show how you feel about each item. If you totally agree, color in the whole circle. If you agree a bit, color in part of the circle. If you don't agree at all, leave the circle blank.

I am glad I told about the sexual abuse.

Abusers know what they are doing is wrong.

My family blames me for the sexual abuse.

Even though people tell me
I'm not to blame, I still feel guilty.

Some people believe the abuser did nothing wrong.

There are people who can help me to feel better.

There are people who can make sure I am safe.

I feel loved and cared for.

Talking about my feelings helps me to feel better.

I believe I am a good person.

I believe I have a happy future.

Chapter 4
Coping With Feelings

PURPOSE OF THE CHAPTER:
Continuing from the theoretical framework of Chapter 3 (which serves as a prerequisite), "Coping With Feelings" introduces the concept of coping skills. This chapter focuses on two underlying principals:
- Knowing what to do with feelings in a constructive and appropriate way provides the child with an important skill in self-care.
- Learning to utilize support systems enables the child to move from "stuck" places emotionally to helpful solutions and the ability to move forward developmentally.

The activities in this chapter are placed in a framework of normative response to stressful situations. Providing opportunities to learn and practice coping skills, the activities are designed to assist children in acquiring skills to deal with the many feelings that may confuse or overwhelm them as a result of their sexual abuse experience, the response to their disclosure, or any aspect they are dealing with in the aftermath of disclosure. These skills have broader applicability and serve as life-skills tools for use in any number of situations.

It is important to note that the authors' framework is one which defines maladaptive coping (i.e., teens who develop substance abuse habits as a way of coping) as a healthy attempt to cope with overwhelming experiences in the absence of effective intervention. In other words, as maladaptive and undesirable as substance abuse is, it is better than a suicide attempt. This framework is noted as an important backdrop for working with adolescents, especially those who may have many maladaptive coping mechanisms. The idea is to accept the present coping style while working to replace it with a healthier coping style.

Latency

Piggy Bank

MODALITY: Individual, group

GOAL: To help children begin to differentiate between comfortable and uncomfortable feelings, and to develop coping strategies to deal with uncomfortable feelings

M A T E R I A L S

➤ Bag

➤ "How Do You Feel When" situations *following*

➤ Flip chart paper

➤ Shoe box (one per child)

➤ Decorative supplies (markers, glitter, colored felt, etc.)

➤ Cardboard cut into coin-sized circles

M E T H O D

ADVANCE PREPARATION:
The therapist copies the "How Do You Feel When" situations onto separate pieces of paper, folds them, and places them in the bag.

ACTIVITY:
The bag is passed around the group and each child must select a

situation from the bag, read the situation aloud, identify the feeling in the situation, and state whether the feeling is a comfortable or uncomfortable feeling to experience. (If done in individual therapy, the therapist and child take turns picking the situations from the bag.)

The therapist then explains, "We all experience comfortable and uncomfortable feelings. Sometimes we feel happy, excited, or relaxed while other times we feel sad, bored, or nervous. It is important to find safe ways to cope with uncomfortable feelings. Let's see how many good ideas we can come up with to deal with uncomfortable feelings." The therapist lists the children's coping ideas onto flip chart paper.

For the next part of the activity, the therapist provides each child with a shoe box to decorate as a piggy bank and cardboard discs to be used as "coins." Children choose coping ideas from the list generated by the group and write each idea onto a coin. A slit is cut into the top of the shoe box. The coins are deposited into the shoe box (the piggy bank). Children can take their piggy banks home and when they are feeling sad, bored, lonely, angry, etc., they can select a coping idea from their bank.

DISCUSSION

Identifying different states of feeling is an important initial step in helping children to express and cope with their strong emotions. This activity will enable children to become aware of different feelings, to understand that feelings are natural, and to realize that they can choose how to cope with uncomfortable feelings.

SITUATIONS:
HOW DO YOU FEEL WHEN...

Somebody teases you.
You win a prize.
You have a bad dream.
Your pet dies.
You are on a roller coaster.
You don't get invited to your classmate's birthday party.
Someone touches your private parts and tells you to keep it a secret.
Your parent reads you a bedtime story.
It's raining and you can't go to the zoo as planned.
You do well on a test.
You get stung by a bee.
It's a day off from school and you have nothing to do.
Your parent buys you a new pair of shoes.
You are daydreaming in class and the teacher scolds you.
Your cat has kittens.
You go to the doctor, who has to give you a shot.
You forget to feed the dog and he goes hungry all day.
Someone offers you money to take a picture of you naked.
You have to read aloud to the class.
You make a new friend.

Latency — Preteen
Coping With Feelings Game

MODALITY: Group

GOAL: To enable children to identify feelings associated with sexual abuse, and to encourage positive coping strategies

MATERIALS

> ➤ 3 pieces of poster board (red, blue and yellow, or any other 3 colors)

> ➤ Scissors

> ➤ Markers

> ➤ Problem Scenarios *following*

METHOD

ADVANCE PREPARATION:
Use three different colors of poster board (red, blue, and yellow). Cut the poster board into 5"x7" rectangular cards. Red is for problem cards; blue for feeling cards; yellow for solution cards. The word *problem* is written onto one side of each red card. The word *feelings* is written onto one side of each blue card. The word *solution* is written onto one side of each yellow card. Cut out the Problem Scenarios and paste one onto the other side of each red card.

Note: Other scenarios can be developed that may be more pertinent to the children in the group. In addition, the leader may wish to have blank cards available for children to make up their own situation cards.

ACTIVITY:

The group sits in a circle. Each player is provided with one problem card, one feeling card, and one solution card. One player begins by reading aloud a problem card. The player to that person's left must then use a feeling card by identifying the feeling(s) in that situation. The next person to the left then uses a solution card by developing a coping strategy for the problem.

Example

Problem: Elizabeth sometimes has nightmares about the sexual abuse.

Feelings: Scared, worried, sad.

Solution: Sleep with a night light on, put a comforting picture beside the bed to look at, draw a picture of the nightmare.

Once a player has used a card, the card is placed in the middle of the circle. The game continues until all players have used their cards.

DISCUSSION

The problem situations in this game are typical dilemmas that sexual victims face. Children have their own experiences validated when they hear read aloud a situation with which they can identify. The game is less threatening because it allows children to problem-solve issues that belong to a fictional character.

Because the game format is appealing to children and allows for equal participation, it is hoped that children who are passive will be encouraged to be more expressive.

PROBLEM SCENARIOS

At Carol's school, they teach kids to say no if someone tries to sexually abuse them. Carol thinks she should have been able to stop the abuse from happening.	Susan told about her uncle sexually abusing her. Now her mother cries all the time.
Kim is glad that the sexual abuse by her grandfather has stopped, but she misses the special way that her grandfather made her feel.	The kids at school found out that Nathan was sexually abused. Now they tease him and they won't play with him.
Barb told her mother that her father had sexually abused her, but her mother is not sure that she believes Barb's story.	Cody has to go to court to testify against the person who sexually abused him. He has never been to court before and he can't stop thinking about it.
While having a bath with her little sister, Amy had thoughts about touching her sister's private parts the way that her step-brother had touched her.	Mary's abuser told her if she ever told anyone about the sexual abuse, he would kill her. Now that she has told, Mary thinks about the abuser coming after her.

PAPER DOLLS AND PAPER AIRPLANES

Latency – Preteen

Acting on My Feelings

MODALITY: Individual, group

GOAL: To normalize feelings and to help children decrease maladaptive behaviors

MATERIALS

➤ Worksheet: "Acting On My Feelings" *following*

METHOD

ADVANCE PREPARATION:
The therapist makes copies of the worksheet to distribute to group members.

ACTIVITY:
Children complete the attached worksheet by drawing happy faces beside those coping strategies that are safe and sad faces beside those coping strategies that are unsafe.

For the second part of the activity, children select two situations from their worksheet (one safe coping strategy and one unsafe coping strategy). Each situation is role-played. The therapist then facilitates a discussion pertaining to the difference between the two coping styles.

The therapist might ask:

- How would a child feel after she has kicked her little brother?
- What might happen to a child who hurts somebody else when she is feeling angry?
- What effect would this have on a child and on her little brother?
- Would a child feel differently if she expresses her anger by punching her pillow?

DISCUSSION

The worksheet and role playing help children to connect their feelings with behavioral expressions. These techniques also help children to further understand the effect that negative reactions have on self and others and to realize the benefits of safe coping strategies. In addition, children with a limited repertoire of safe coping strategies can learn more effective methods of dealing with their feelings. Ultimately, the therapeutic goal is to enable children to openly discuss their thoughts and feelings rather than to act them out inappropriately.

WORKSHEET

ACTING ON
MY FEELINGS

Kids usually have many different feelings after they have been sexually abused—sad, mad, confused. Sometimes it's hard to know what to do with all these mixed-up feelings. It is OK to have these feelings, but it is not OK to do something that will hurt yourself or someone else. It is important to find safe ways to show your feelings. Below is a list of ways to show your feelings. Put a happy face beside the safe ways to show feelings and a sad face beside the unsafe ways to show feelings.

When I feel angry, I kick my little brother.

When I feel lonely, I hug my teddy bear.

When I feel angry, I do a silent scream or I scream out loud.

When I feel sad, I cry.

When I feel rejected or left out,
I make fun of other kids.

When I feel angry, I punch my pillow.

When I feel lonely, I call a friend..

When I feel hurt, I hurt other people.

When I feel confused, I ask questions.

When I feel sad, I hug myself.

When I feel angry, I bang my head against a wall.

When I feel upset, I talk to an adult I trust.

When I feel _____,
I _____.

Preteen — Teen

Stressed Out

MODALITY: Individual, group

GOALS: To promote a better understanding of how people deal with stress, anger, and uncomfortable feelings; to identify personal warning signs of stress; to acquire strategies for coping with stress

MATERIALS

➤ Questionnaire: "Signs of Stress" *following*

➤ "Stress Map" *following*

➤ Pens

➤ Stickers (5/16" diameter color coding labels are excellent for this purpose. They are readily available from office supply stores.)

➤ "Stress Management" game *following*

METHOD

ADVANCE PREPARATION:

The therapist should make copies of the questionnaire and the "Stress Map." Provide pens and stickers. Make a copy of the "Stress Management" game to use with several players. The therapist should make a large sketch of a human torso on a flip chart or chalkboard. Include arrows to the relevant organs (hypothalamus, eyes, lungs, heart, stomach, skin and blood vessels) as shown on the next page.

STRESS MAP

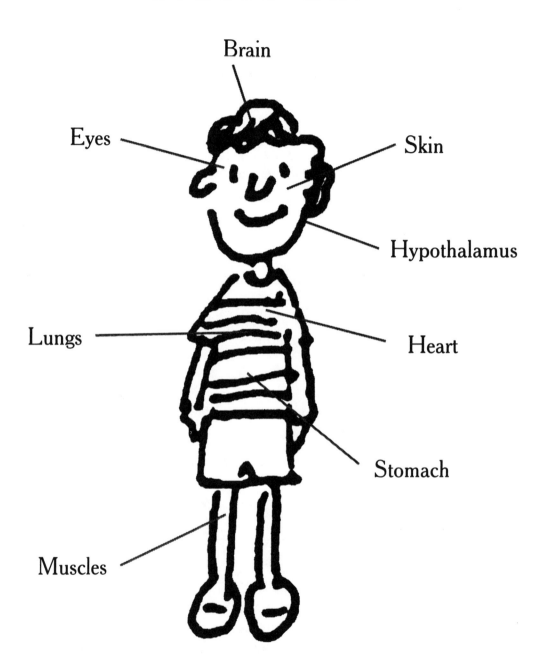

Brain

Eyes

Skin

Hypothalamus

Lungs

Heart

Stomach

Muscles

ACTIVITY:

The therapist reads the following news item which is an excellent example of an extremely stressful situation and then asks the group how something like this can happen.

MOTHER LIFTS CAR TO SAVE CHILD

A three-year-old girl is listed in good condition at Vancouver Community Hospital today, after her 130-pound mother lifted a 2,000 pound car from the child's pinned legs.

According to police, Jennifer Palmer was playing near her driveway at about 2:00 p.m. yesterday afternoon when a parked car rolled and crashed into the Palmer home, trapping the toddler under the wheels. Caroline Palmer, 25, heard the crash and rushed from the house to her daughter's rescue.

"I didn't think," Mrs. Palmer said at the hospital this morning. "I screamed and ran toward her and lifted the car off her." The child suffered two broken legs, but managed to pull herself from beneath the car. Onlookers were astonished to see the young mother lift the car without any help.

The discussion can be broadened to identify other kinds of stressful situations. Disclosing and dealing with sexual abuse can be included in a list of extremely stressful situations.

The therapist then uses the diagram to give a brief and simple explanation of the body's reaction to stress; i.e., when our bodies are exposed to stressful situations, an "alert signal" flashes to the brain.

STRESS AFFECTS THE BODY

HYPOTHALAMUS   small bunch of nerve cells at
the base of the brain — the central
command station that releases specific
hormones (body chemicals)

STOMACH   digestion stops or slows down, bladder
and rectal muscles relax

HEART   rate increases

SKIN   perspiration increases

LUNGS   breathing gets faster

BLOOD VESSELS   blood pressure increases
vessels dilate
blood clots move rapidly

MUSCLES   tensed, ready for fight or flight

EYES   pupils dilate

The leader explains that sexual abuse is very stressful to children.
Kids are afraid of many aspects of what has happened, what is now
happening, and what will happen in the future.

After the group members have been given some basic information
about stress and physiological reactions to stress, they can begin to
identify their own signs of stress.

At this point in the activity, the leader distributes a copy of the "Stress
Map" and stickers. Group members then apply the stickers to their
maps to identify where their bodies feel stress.

After each group member completes his or her map, they can be shared with the group. As an alternative or an additional assessment tool, group members can complete the "Signs of Stress" questionnaire.

Next, the therapist can ask the group for their ideas about the stress all children who have been sexually abused experience. Stressors can include lists of worries and fears, the stress of anticipating seeing an offender, the strain of keeping the secret of sexual abuse.

The next part of the activity consists of having the group share strategies for coping with stress and the symptoms of stress. The leader participates in this part of the activity by offering sample strategies: guided imagery, relaxation tapes.

The final part of this activity is to have members develop a personalized stress kit with such items as bath salts, a daily planner/organizer, exercise routine, a pillow to punch, distress center phone number, etc.

As a closing activity, group members can play the "Stress Management" game.

DISCUSSION

Managing stress is an essential component of recovering from the trauma of sexual abuse. It is also a preventative measure which group members can utilize in any stressful situation or life crisis. This activity can take several sessions to complete. The strategies can be practiced individually and incorporated into each group session.

QUESTIONNAIRE

SIGNS OF STRESS

NEVER **A LITTLE** **A LOT**

☐ ☐ ☐ I get headaches.

☐ ☐ ☐ I feel nauseous or have an upset stomach.

☐ ☐ ☐ My back hurts.

☐ ☐ ☐ I get skin rashes.

☐ ☐ ☐ I feel tired all the time.

☐ ☐ ☐ I often have muscle aches.

☐ ☐ ☐ I have a pounding heart at times.

☐ ☐ ☐ I've had a change in appetite.

☐ ☐ ☐ I get diarrhea.

☐ ☐ ☐ I have a problem with constipation.

☐ ☐ ☐ I have trouble falling asleep.

☐ ☐ ☐ I sweat a lot.

☐ ☐ ☐ My hands shake.

SIGNS OF STRESS

NEVER	A LITTLE	A LOT	
☐	☐	☐	I get dizzy.
☐	☐	☐	I can't get a deep breath sometimes.
☐	☐	☐	I feel restless.
☐	☐	☐	I am irritable or cranky.
☐	☐	☐	I feel anxious.
☐	☐	☐	I feel angry (mad at the world).
☐	☐	☐	I feel I don't care about things.
☐	☐	☐	I'm bored.
☐	☐	☐	I can't get rid of guilt — it's always with me.
☐	☐	☐	I have poor concentration.
☐	☐	☐	I have mood swings.
☐	☐	☐	I can't stop touching my hair, ears, nose (or other body parts).

SIGNS OF STRESS

NEVER	A LITTLE	A LOT	
☐	☐	☐	I drink alcohol or use drugs.
☐	☐	☐	I bite my lips.
☐	☐	☐	I tap my foot.
☐	☐	☐	I seem to do things quickly, without thinking.
☐	☐	☐	I grind my teeth.
☐	☐	☐	I've been pulling away from family or friends; I just don't feel like being with people.
☐	☐	☐	I bite my nails.
☐	☐	☐	I feel disconnected.
☐	☐	☐	I have a short fuse or over-react.
☐	☐	☐	I think about hurting myself.
☐	☐	☐	I smoke to calm down.

MAP

STRESS MAP

Use stickers to pinpoint where you feel stress in your body.

GAME

STRESS MANAGEMENT

Each player uses coins as game markers and dice. Flip the coin to advance. Heads means you move ahead one space. Tails means two spaces. When you land on a spot, follow the directions. First one to finish is stress free.

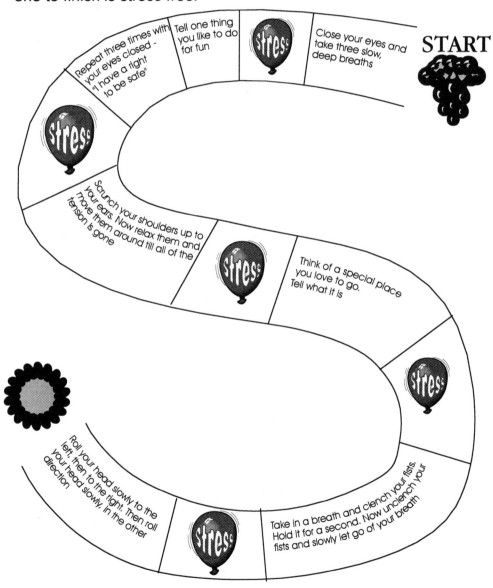

Preteen – Teen
Balancing Scale

MODALITY: Individual, group

GOAL: To normalize coping strategies and to help teens alter their patterns of self-abusive behavior

MATERIALS

➤ Questionnaire: "Coping Strategies" *following*

➤ Handout: "Evaluating My Coping Strategies"

➤ Worksheet: "Balancing Scale" *following*

METHOD

ADVANCE PREPARATION:
The group leader copies the questionnaire, the handout, and the worksheet to use with the children.

ACTIVITY:
The therapist introduces this activity by stating: "Most people engage in self-abusive behavior, whether it is drinking too much coffee, nail biting, smoking, etc. We do these things in order to cope. This behavior helps us in some ways and harms us in other ways. People who have been sexually abused often cope with the pain by getting involved in behavior that is self-abusive. It is important to evaluate how this behavior is helpful and how it is not helpful, so that a choice can be made about whether to continue the behavior or look for other

ways to cope. First, let's see which strategies you're using to cope with the sexual abuse, then we'll evaluate how these strategies are helping and not helping you."

The child completes the questionnaire on "coping strategies." The child chooses one of the coping strategies she or he circled on the questionnaire and writes it at the top of the page on the balancing scale worksheet..

Using the "Evaluating My Coping Strategies" worksheet, the child cuts out the ways in which the coping strategy helps and places these on the left side of the "Balancing Scale" worksheet. The child then cuts out how the coping strategy does not help and places these on the right side of the "Balancing Scale" worksheet. The child is encouraged to add other coping strategies and whether they help or do not help.

At the end, the child can see which side of the scale has more weight: the "help" side or the "don't help" side.

The next step is for the client to make a list of coping strategies that will be helpful, such as talking to a trusted person, keeping a journal, or going into the hospital for a break.

DISCUSSION

This activity is to be used with teens who are engaging in self-abusive behavior. The activity involves three steps: identifying coping strategies, evaluating these strategies, and brainstorming alternate ways of coping.

The therapist should be cautioned not to reinforce the idea that the child is "bad" for getting involved in acts of self-harm. Rather, the therapist should help teens feel a sense of control and empowerment by recognizing that they can choose how to cope with the sexual abuse.

QUESTIONNAIRE

IDENTIFYING COPING STRATEGIES

People who have been sexually abused cope with the pain in different ways. Put checks beside the ways that you cope.

- ☐ Smoke
- ☐ Drink alcohol
- ☐ Use drugs
- ☐ Cut myself
- ☐ Burn myself
- ☐ Overeat
- ☐ Don't eat
- ☐ Force myself to vomit after I eat
- ☐ Sleep a lot
- ☐ Don't sleep enough
- ☐ Avoid close relationships
- ☐ Avoid sex
- ☐ Have sex a lot more than I think is normal
- ☐ Run away
- ☐ Do weird things without thinking
- ☐ Other _____
- ☐ Other _____
- ☐ Other _____

HANDOUT

EVALUATING MY COPING STRATEGIES

HOW MY COPING STRATEGIES HELP ME	HOW MY COPING STRATEGIES DON'T HELP ME
Makes sure I get help	Makes me feel worse about myself
Keeps the abuser away	Hurts me
Attracts attention	Makes me feel crazy
Gives me a feeling of control	Gets me in trouble
Keeps me alive	Makes people think I'm weird
Makes me feel happy	Is bad for my health
Makes me feel special	Keeps people away
Gets my mind off my worries	Punishes me or others
Gets the anger out	Hurts others I care about
Gets the sadness out	Keeps me from trusting people
Keeps me busy	Prevents me from achieving
Makes my problems seem smaller	Makes my problems worse
Releases tension	Isolates me
Gets me through the day	Takes pleasure out of my life
Other:	Other:
Other:	Other:
Other:	Other:

BALANCING SCALE

HELPS ME   DOESN'T HELP ME

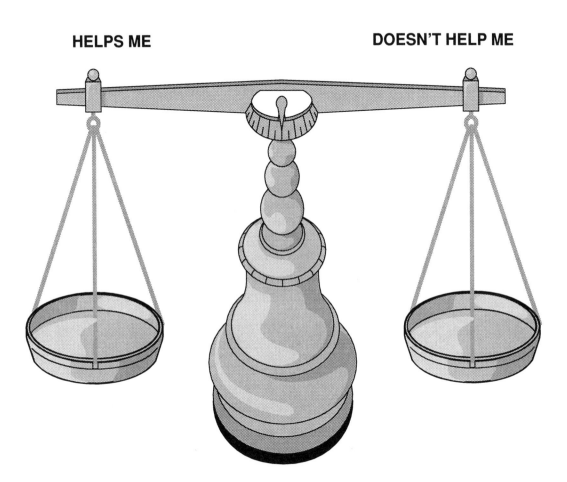

Preteen — Teen
Runaway Train

MODALITY: Individual, group

GOAL: To enable sexual victims to identify feelings and coping strategies associated with the sexual abuse

MATERIALS

➤ Flip chart paper

➤ Song: "Runaway Train" by Soul Asylum (Sony Music)

➤ Guided fantasy script *following*

➤ Paper and coloring supplies

METHOD

ADVANCE PREPARATION:
Find a recording of the song. Prepare a quiet area for the guided fantasy experience.

ACTIVITY:
The group leader plays the song "Runaway Train" for the group. The group is then asked to identify and discuss the various feelings that are in the song and the coping strategies used by the person in the song. The therapist states that similar to the song, sexual abuse victims may have many different feelings associated with the abuse that can be

confusing and overwhelming; and victims may use various coping strategies to run away from the emotional pain.

The group generates a list of feelings that victims of sexual abuse may have, and the coping strategies used to deal with the feelings. The group leader facilitates a discussion about safe and unsafe coping styles.

This is followed by a guided fantasy exercise in which group members are helped to imagine a journey to a safe place. Once the guided fantasy is completed, group members can write about or draw their safe place. As an alternative, group members can write postcards to one another from their "safe place." They tell one another what their safe place is like, how it feels to be there, etc.

DISCUSSION

Sexual abuse victims often are overwhelmed by strong emotions. They may involve themselves in self-abusive behavior in order to cope and to gain control. Guided imagery and relaxation exercises can help children feel a sense of calmness. Although guided imagery exercises can be a useful tool for teens to add to their repertoire of coping strategies, the therapist should be aware that some group members will have difficulty concentrating and relaxing.

Note: It is recommended that therapists have some knowledge and experience of guided imagery exercises before using this activity with clients. Therapists can refer to the book, *Creative Visualization* (Gawain, 1995).

GUIDED FANTASY

JOURNEY TO A SAFE PLACE

(To be read aloud slowly and clearly to the group. Allow pauses so group members can reach a relaxed state and have time to visualize their safe place.)

Lie on your back or sit comfortably in a chair with your palms facing upwards. Uncross your legs and arms and allow your body to relax naturally. Let the full weight of your body relax. Breathe in and slowly exhale. Do this several times until you feel your body begin to relax.... Breathe out any tension or anxiety. Ask your body to let go and just relax....

Imagine that you are getting ready for a train ride. You are going on a journey to a safe place.

Imagine yourself packing a suitcase for this trip. What would you need for your journey of healing? You may want to take someone that you can talk to along the way—a trusted friend, a close family member, a therapist. Take a few moments and think of other things that you would need to take on your journey.

Now that you are packed and ready to go, imagine yourself getting on the train. You slowly climb the stairs and enter the train. You sit down in a big, comfortable, cozy seat. As you sit down, you can feel your whole body sink into the softness of the chair. Your whole body feels relaxed.

The train begins to move, slowly gliding along. You feel as if you are floating gently and peacefully toward a place of tranquillity. Take time to enjoy the slow, peaceful ride....The sun fills the train car with soothing warm light. Your body fills with warmth from the top of your head to the tips of your toes. Allow yourself to feel this warmth.... You breathe in peacefulness. The train approaches its destination. You begin to feel more and more peaceful and calm.

Now imagine yourself in this safe place. Take time to feel what is around you.... Breath in and smell the tranquil air.... Listen to the comforting sounds.... Take a few moments to visualize your place of safety. It's a place where you feel at peace, secure, and in control.....

Now slowly and whenever you feel ready, allow your mind to return to the room. You slowly begin to feel your surroundings, hear the sounds, smell the room, touch the floor beneath you... Whenever you feel ready, you may open your eyes.

All Ages
Dream Pillows

MODALITY: Individual, group

GOAL: To address night terrors and fears; to develop coping strategies to deal with nightmares

MATERIALS

> ➤ Fabric remnants (select patterns with stars, moons, etc.)

> ➤ Gold thread

> ➤ Cardboard pieces of various sizes

> ➤ Cotton batting

> ➤ Fabric glue

> ➤ Hole punch

> ➤ Darning needles

> ➤ Wool

> ➤ Colorful fabric tape

> ➤ "Dream Survey" *following*

METHOD

ADVANCE PREPARATION:
The therapist must assemble the listed materials. The therapist also prepares some simple questions concerning bedtime rituals and then writes each question on a card (sample questions are provided for each age group) The cards are placed facedown in the center of the group.

ACTIVITY:

This activity has three parts. The first part helps children become aware of their existing sleeping patterns and habits. The second part provides an opportunity to express scary dreams and nightmares. The third part offers children some skills to master their fears.

The therapist introduces the activity by explaining that everyone has a special routine for getting ready to sleep or rest. Sometimes we are not aware of all our rituals. The therapist explains that the cards are a survey of bedtime rituals.

Each group member then takes a turn drawing a card from the stack and reading it to the group. This survey approach allows the leader to introduce the topic of nightmares, scary dreams, and night terrors.

Each group member then writes or draws about a scary dream. It is best to give several options. Some children and teens prefer to draw a picture of their dreams. Others are more comfortable writing about their dreams.

Group members are then invited to discuss their nightmares and exchange ways of dealing with scary dreams.

DREAM PILLOWS:

The final part of the activity consists of having the group make dream pillows. It is a good idea to have a pillow constructed in advance for the group members to see. A small quantity of cotton batting is placed on a piece of cardboard. Then a piece of fabric slightly larger than the cardboard is cut and glued over the cotton batting so that it resembles a pillow. Use lots of glue, or tape securely with fabric tape all around the edges. For extra durability, the group leader or caregiver can sew the pillow using darning needles and wool. Poems and sayings about dreams can be copied onto the reverse side of the pillow. Caregivers and group leaders can write positive thoughts on the children's dream pillows, such as: "sweet dreams!"

DISCUSSION

Nightmares are very common and frightening events for sexually abused children. Learning about dreaming can be very reassuring. Group members usually help each other by sharing techniques for coping with nightmares.

They may offer suggestions such as:

- Turn on the radio.

- Use a night light.

- Leave a comforting snack on the bedside table.

- Read for a little while.

- Invent a dream friend (like your dog, best friend, or a special superhero). Have your dream friend enter your dream and face your scary monsters with you.

DREAM SURVEY

PRESCHOOL

Do you have a favorite nighttime treat?	Do you have a bedtime story?
Do you say a nighttime prayer?	Do you like a lullaby?
Do you like to be tucked in?	Who says good night to you?
Do you sleep with a teddy bear?	

DREAM SURVEY

LATENCY AND PRETEENS

Do you have a nighttime treat?	Do you sleep with a stuffed animal?
Do you read a story?	Do you sleep with a nightlight?
Do you write in your diary?	Do you take a warm bath before bedtime?
Do you say good night to people in your home?	What things make you feel safe and comfortable before you drift off to sleep?
What time is your regular bedtime?	How many hours do you sleep each night?

DREAM SURVEY

TEENS

Do you have a favorite snack at bedtime?	Do you listen to music before you fall asleep?
How many pillows do you sleep with?	Do you take a warm bath before bedtime?
What do you wear to bed?	Do you have a special way of relaxing in the hour before you go to bed?
What time do you usually fall asleep?	Do you read before falling asleep?
What is your favorite sleeping position?	Do you set an alarm to wake up?

DREAM PILLOWS

Sweet dreams little one!

All Ages
Calendars

MODALITY: Individual, group

GOAL: To encourage appropriate self-care

MATERIALS

➤ Worksheet: "Be Good to Yourself Everyday" *following*

➤ Blank calendar *following*

➤ Scissors

➤ Glue

➤ Decorative supplies (markers, glitter, stickers, etc.)

METHOD

ADVANCE PREPARATION:
Make copies of the worksheet and blank calendar to use with the children. The "31 Ways to Nurture Your Child" can be copied and distributed to parents.

ACTIVITY:
Each child is provided with a "Be Good to Yourself Every Day" worksheet as well as a blank calendar. Children select 31 of the 49 ideas on the worksheet, cut them out, and glue them in any desired order on their calendars. Children can use the markers and stickers to

decorate their calendars. Children can take the calendars home and follow the daily instructions.

This activity can be adapted for use in a preschool/non-offending parent's group by handing out the "31 Ways to Nurture Your Child" calendars and having group members decorate them.

DISCUSSION

Rather than giving the children calendars with pre-selected ideas, this activity allows children to choose the items and to make their own calendars. Thus, children are empowered to involve themselves in self-care activities.

BE GOOD TO YOURSELF EVERY DAY

Look in the mirror and remind yourself you have a nice smile.	Take a warm bath.	Ask someone for a hug.	Do something fun and outrageous.	Read the comics from the newspaper.	Tell a friend about something special that happened this week.	Bake a batch of cookies.
Show your kindness by doing something nice for somebody.	Think about a nice thought as you are falling asleep tonight.	Give yourself a hug.	Find a tree and name it after yourself.	Whistle a happy tune.	Remind yourself about something you are proud of.	Write a letter to someone.
Drink something warm and soothing.	Think about something that you are good at.	Sing a verse of your favorite song.	Blow the biggest bubble that you can with a piece of gum.	Laughter makes us feel good. Make a funny face in the mirror.	Hold something soft and cuddly.	Make grape juice mustaches.
Give yourself a gift.	Make a list of your favorite things.	Give yourself a favorite food treat.	Take a moment to smell something nice.	Express yourself! Write your thoughts down in a journal.	Remind yourself of something you have achieved.	Make a picture and put it on the fridge.
Decorate a sign for your bedroom door.	Make up an exercise routine.	Dress up as your favorite fairy tale character.	Plan an orange day; wear orange and eat something orange.	Pack a lunch and have an indoor picnic.	Go outside and watch the clouds. Make a picture of what you see.	Rub nice smelling lotion on your hands.
Draw/write an ending for a bad dream you had.	See how many times you can hit a balloon in the air without it landing.	Let out your stress. Punch a pillow ten times.	Write a letter to yourself and save it to read on a rainy day.	Draw a picture of a favorite place you have been to.	Hide a luckypenny outside for someone to find.	Make a paper airplane and see how far you can throw it.
Make a musical instrument from household items.	Rub baby powder on your feet and make footprints on black paper.	Trade a book with a friend and curl up on the couch to read it.	You are a superstar! Cut out stars and hang them from your ceiling.	Put on some music and dance around your room.	Try something you have never done before.	There is nobody else exactly like you. Remind yourself you are special!

BE GOOD TO YOURSELF EVERY DAY

SUNDAY	MONDAY	TUESDAY	WEDNESDAY	THURSDAY	FRIDAY	SATURDAY

31 WAYS TO NURTURE YOUR CHILD

SUNDAY	MONDAY	TUESDAY	WEDNESDAY	THURSDAY	FRIDAY	SATURDAY
1. Tell your child you love her or him.	2. Hide a lucky penny for your child to find..	3. Give your child a hug.	4. Read your child a bed-time story.	5. Tell your child how special he or she is to you.	6. Rub body lotion on your child's hands.	7. Bake cookies together.
8. Play a board game with your child.	9. Play in the snow, leaves or sand together.	10. Bake a cake to celebrate how special your child is to you.	11. Sing a song to your child.	12. Talk to your child about what a wonderful baby he or she was.	13. Take your child on a nature walk.	14. Praise your child's beautiiful smile.
15. Look at the family album together and talk about the pictures.	16. Make your child's favorite meal for dinner.	17. Talk to your child about a special memory you share together.	18. Make your child a warm, soothing drink.	19. Give your child something cuddly to hold.	20. Go to the library together.	21. Put a picture of your child beside your bed or on your desk.
22. Give your child a foot tickle.	23. Point out something you think is really special about your child.	24. Put your child's drawings on the fridge.	25. Play dress-up with your child	26. Put a loving note in your child's lunch box.	27. Walk through the park with your child and feed the ducks.	28. Give your child an Eskimo kiss (rub noses).
29. Go swimming together.	30. Push your child on a swing at the school or park playground.	31. Tell your child you love her or him again and again.				

Chapter 5
Secrets

PURPOSE OF THE CHAPTER:

When doing activities about secrets, it is important to acknowledge the many reasons children keep the sexual abuse a secret. Some children keep the secret because they worry about the repercussions of their disclosure. They think that they won't be believed or they will get in trouble; that the abuser will harm them; that the family will be torn apart etc. In order to help alleviate the victim's feelings of guilt for having kept the abuse a secret, treatment interventions need to validate how hard it is for children to disclose the abuse.

Children may also keep the abuse a secret because of threats made by the abuser. Various levels of coercion may have been utilized to keep the child silent. Whether the threat was covert or overt, it is important to understand how the offender succeeded in maintaining the child's secrecy. This issue is sometimes closely related to the child's concept of why he or she was chosen by the offender. (For example, "He knew I wouldn't tell.") If this belief is not fully explored, the child can develop feelings of self-hate as well as self-blame.

Another dynamic to be particularly aware of is that of the child keeping the secret to protect someone else. It is important to help victims understand that secrecy is a key element in sexually abusive relationships. The therapeutic challenge is to enable children to understand the function of the secret. (Sexual abusers get kids to keep the abuse a secret so they can maintain control and avoid getting caught.) It is also important to re-frame the secrecy for each child and to help them reconstruct their experience, enabling them to externalize the conflict of having kept the secret.

Preschool
Keeping the Secret

MODALITY: Individual, group

GOAL: To help children understand the elements of secrecy involved in child sexual abuse and to differentiate between safe and unsafe secrets

MATERIALS

➤ Bag filled with candy

➤ Activity Book: "Secrets" (one per child) *following*

➤ 2 kinds of stickers (for example, happy faces for safe secrets; bees for unsafe secrets)

METHOD

ADVANCE PREPARATION:
Bring a bag filled with candy to the session. Make copies of the activity book for each child.

The therapist introduces the concept of secrets by holding a bag filled with candy and asking the children to guess what is in the bag. Once the children have guessed, the treat is shared with the group. The therapist then asks the children if they think this was a fun, safe secret or a scary, unsafe secret. This leads into a discussion of safe and unsafe secrets, and children are invited to give examples. It is important for the therapist to explain that some secrets may start off as fun and turn into scary or confusing unsafe secrets, such as when an offender bribes the child with a chocolate bar then involves the child in secret touching.

The therapist provides each child with the "Secrets" activity book to complete. The adult care givers can read the booklets to the children, and the children can follow along by coloring the pictures and completing the activities.

DISCUSSION

Young children must first grasp the meaning of what a secret is before they can discern between a safe and an unsafe secret. The coloring book will help children understand the difference between safe and unsafe secrets. Children will learn that it is OK to keep good or fun secrets, but not OK to keep secrets that are harmful. Jan Hindman's *A Very Touching Book* can be helpful in emphasizing concepts related to secrets and secret touching.

Note: This activity is rather lengthy for young children, so the therapist may wish to do the activity over two sessions. As an alternative, the last part of the activity (in which children place stickers beside safe and unsafe scenarios) can be done with the larger group. The scenarios can be copied onto large poster board and taped to the wall, and children can take turns showing which scenarios are safe or unsafe by placing the stickers onto the poster board.

ACTIVITY BOOK

SECRETS

A secret is when you know something and you don't tell other people about it. Some secrets are OK to keep because they are fun, and nobody gets hurt. Like if you have a penny collection and you hide the penny collection in a secret place in your bedroom so nobody else knows where to find it. Safe secrets are fun and exciting to keep! Color in the face below to show how kids feel when they have a safe secret.

Other secrets are unsafe secrets because they make you feel scared, hurt, yucky, or mixed-up. Like if your brother goes to play near the train tracks where it is very dangerous and he tells you not to tell your parents. Unsafe secrets are not OK to keep, even if someone makes you promise not to tell. You should always tell an adult about unsafe secrets. Unsafe secrets are scary or dangerous to keep. Color in the face below to show how kids feel when they have an unsafe secret.

ACTIVITY BOOK

When somebody touches your private body parts or makes you touch their private body parts and then makes you promise not to tell, this is called *secret touching* and this is an unsafe secret. It may be hard to tell an adult about secret touching because you may feel confused if you were told not to tell; or you may feel scared about what will happen if you tell. You were very, very, very brave because you helped the secret to come out! Draw a picture of the person you told about the secret touching.

Now let's practice telling the difference between a safe secret that is OK to keep and an unsafe secret that is NOT OK to keep. For each situation below, put a happy face sticker if it is a safe secret that is OK to keep, or put a bee sticker if it is a scary or confusing secret that is not OK to keep.

Your parents bought you a gigantic stuffed animal and kept it a secret until your birthday.

A child at the park steals another child's bike and tells you not to tell anybody.

Your baby-sitter makes you touch her private body parts and makes you promise not to tell.

Your grandmother bakes a yummy chocolate cake and hides it until it is time to eat dessert.

Your cousin asks you to play a game called "sex" and tells you to take your clothes off. She says if you tell anyone she won't be your friend any more.

Your big brother takes you to a secret fort and tells you the secret password to get in, but you are not to tell anyone else.

Your best friend tells you that her uncle touches her private parts, and she tells you it is a secret and you can't tell anyone.

You make a beautiful card for your mother and you hide it until Mother's Day.

Latency – Preteen
Ghostwriter

MODALITY: Group

GOAL: To help children understand the elements of secrecy
               involved in child sexual abuse

MATERIALS

➤ Three envelopes and strips of paper

➤ Invisible ink markers (ghost writers and developers are
   available at toy stores)

METHOD

ADVANCE PREPARATION:
The therapist should write on the outside of one envelope: "Children
keep the sexual abuse a secret because..." On the outside of the
second envelope, write: "Abusers trick kids into keeping the sexual
abuse a secret because..." The answers to these questions are written
in invisible ink on separate pieces of paper (see following), folded,
and placed in the appropriate envelopes. The envelopes are then
sealed.

Note: If invisible ink markers and developers are unavailable, then
the following process can be used: write the secret message on white
paper using blue-colored pencil. Use a red-colored pencil to scribble
over the message so that it is concealed. The message can be seen by

placing red cellophane over it.

ACTIVITY:

The activity begins by having each child write down a secret on a strip of paper and placing it in the third envelope. For added appeal, the secrets can be written using the invisible ink "ghost writers."

This envelope is passed around to group members who each take out a "secret." Each child uses the "ghost developer" marker to uncover what is written on his strip of paper. The secrets, read aloud to the group are used as a basis for discussion on the concept of secrets.

For the next part of the activity, the group leader announces that there are two envelopes that have a message written on them with the secret answers on the inside. The therapist presents the first envelope to the group and states, "There are many reasons why kids keep the sexual abuse a secret. Some of the reasons are in this secret envelope."

The envelope is then opened and, as it is passed around the group, each child pulls a paper strip from the envelope. Group members use the "ghost developer" to uncover what is written on the slip of paper. These are read to the rest of the group.

The second envelope is introduced by the group leader who states, "Kids are usually tricked by the abuser into keeping the abuse a secret because the abuser doesn't want people to find out what he or she has done. Some of the reasons are in this secret envelope."

The envelope is passed around and group members take turns pulling a strip of paper from the envelope, using the ghost developer to uncover the message, and reading the statement aloud to the group. Group members can then discuss their own personal experiences of why they kept the secret and why they believe their abuser made them keep the abuse a secret.

DISCUSSION

Victims of child sexual abuse typically have feelings of guilt associated with having kept the sexual abuse a secret. In order to help alleviate these feelings of guilt, children need help in understanding that secrecy is a part of the sexually abusive relationship, and there are reasons why abusers want kids to maintain the secrecy.

KEEPING THE SEXUAL ABUSE A SECRET

KIDS KEEP THE SEXUAL ABUSE A SECRET BECAUSE...

➤ The abuser told them not to tell.

➤ They are worried about what will happen if they tell.

➤ They feel that the abuse is their fault.

➤ They think it is their job to protect the abuser.

➤ They think it is their job to protect someone else, like a parent or a sibling.

➤ They feel too ashamed to tell anyone.

➤ They worry about what people will think about them if they tell.

➤ Having a secret to keep makes them feel special.

➤ They fear that they will not be believed.

➤ They feel helpless, that nobody will be able to do anything about it.

ABUSERS TRICK KIDS INTO KEEPING THE ABUSE A SECRET BECAUSE...

➤ They do not want to get in trouble.

➤ They want to be in control.

➤ They want to avoid going to jail.

➤ They would feel ashamed if people found out about what they did.

➤ They know that people would believe the child.

➤ They can continue to abuse the child if people don't know about it.

➤ They do not want to have to leave their family.

➤ They know that sexual abuse is a crime.

Latency – Preteen

Secret Puzzle

MODALITY: Individual, group

GOAL: To help children understand the elements of secrecy involved in child sexual abuse and to help children differentiate between safe and unsafe secrets

MATERIALS

➤ "Secret Puzzle" (one per child) *following*

METHOD

ADVANCE PREPARATION:
Copy both sides of the "Secret Puzzle" onto one piece of cardboard or heavy colored paper. Then cut the puzzle along the dotted lines and place the six pieces in an envelope.

The therapist introduces the idea of secrecy by dividing the group into pairs and having the pairs create their own "secret handshake." (If this activity is being done in individual therapy, then the therapist and child can develop the handshake.) The group leader facilitates a discussion about what it is like to have a secret handshake and how a secret like this is different from the secret of sexual abuse.

The therapist provides each child with a "Secret Puzzle" (see following). The children complete the puzzle by writing a response to each of the six questions. The child completes the puzzle by beginning with number 1 and progressing to number 6. Once each piece of the puzzle has been completed, the child can assemble the puzzle and tape it together. The child can then turn the puzzle to the other side to uncover the secret message.

DISCUSSION

This activity focuses on elements of secrecy as well as factors associated with disclosure. The "secret message" provides a positive affirmation of the victim's disclosure, resulting in the child feeling empowered about having told the secret.

Many sexual victims experience strong feelings of guilt and shame for having kept the abuse a secret. Children's feelings will be eased when they hear that fellow group members also kept the abuse a secret. The therapist also plays a pivotal role in alleviating the children's feelings of guilt and shame by highlighting the many reasons why victims typically maintain the secrecy of sexual abuse. For example, the therapist can say, "Kids often keep the sexual abuse a secret because they worry about what will happen if they tell, or because they are too embarrassed to talk about it. It's important that you know lots of kids feel the same way you do."

PUZZLE

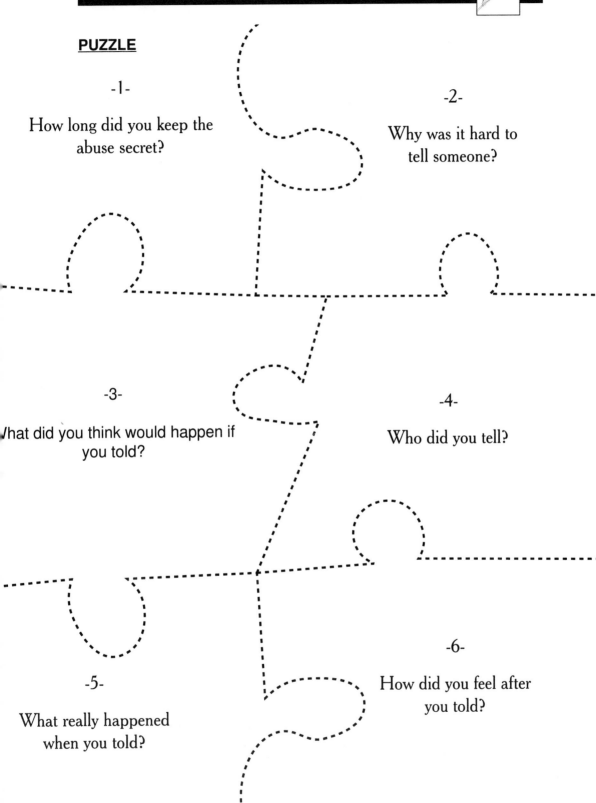

-1-

How long did you keep the
abuse secret?

-2-

Why was it hard to
tell someone?

-3-

What did you think would happen if
you told?

-4-

Who did you tell?

-5-

What really happened
when you told?

-6-

How did you feel after
you told?

YOU WERE

BRAVE

TO HAVE TOLD

ABOUT THE

SEXUAL ABUSE!

Latency-Teen
Target

MODALITY: Individual, group

GOALS: To validate and affirm children's bravery in disclosing sexual abuse; to break down feelings of isolation and alienation created by secrecy; to help group members gain understanding of the offender's misuse of trust to ensure compliance and secrecy

---

M A T E R I A L S

➤ Set of question cards

➤ Sponge or soft ball

➤ Small pail of water

➤ Poster board

➤ "Secret Code" *following*

➤ Index cards

M E T H O D

ADVANCE PREPARATION:

Copy each question from the "question cards" list onto separate index cards. To make the target, color a large piece of poster board 2 different colors. One color represents "ask a question" and the other color represents "answer a question".

ACTIVITY:

This game can be played like a game of darts. Group members take turns dipping a sponge into water and throwing it at the target. If a player hits "ask a question," they pick a question card from the stack of index cards and are entitled to ask any group member the question that was picked. If they hit "answer a question," they must give the answer to the question themselves. If a card selected is too difficult for an individual to answer, ask the group members to assist. This will model asking for help and getting support from peers.

The sexual abuse content is focused on Secrets and leads easily into a discussion of the role secrecy plays in sexual abuse.

The last part of the activity can include "secret codes." The leader hands out a Secret Code sheet to each group member. Group members decipher the message, "Sexual abuse is never a kid's fault." Children of all ages will enjoy sending each other secret messages of support as a closing activity.

DISCUSSION

Secrecy is an important issue for all sexual abuse victims. This activity gives recognition to both how difficult it is for children to keep the secret and how difficult it is to disclose the secret.

The activity gives children an opportunity to approach secrecy in a playful way. It works particularly well with boys who find it awkward and difficult to talk about this topic. The game format provides some release of tension for a highly charged subject.

Following the game, the therapist can facilitate a discussion about the activity and identify commonalities among group members.

QUESTION CARDS

How long did you keep the secret?	Why is it hard to talk about abuse?
Who did you tell first?	How did the offender try to make you keep the secret?
What happened when you told about the sexual abuse?	Why did you pick the person that you told?
What's the worst thing about telling about sexual abuse?	What would you do if someone confided in you that she was being sexually abused and made you promise not to tell?
What's the best thing about telling about sexual abuse?	What should a kid who tells about being abused do when the person they tell doesn't believe them?
Why are kids never to blame for sexual abuse?	Why do offenders try to make kids keep the sexual abuse a secret?

SECRET CODE

Use the code below to spell out this important message.

EXAMPLE   3 1 20 = CAT

| 1 | A | 2 | B | 3 | C | 4 | D | 5 | E | 6 | F | 7 | G | 8 | H | 9 | I | 10 | J | 11 | K | 12 | L | 13 | M | 14 | N | 15 | O | 16 | P |
| 17 | Q | 18 | R | 19 | S | 20 | T | 21 | U | 22 | V | 23 | W | 24 | X | 25 | Y | 26 | Z |

BREAK THIS CODE

| 19 5 24 21 1 12 | 1 2 21 19 5 | 9 19 |
| 14 5 22 5 18 | 11 9 4 19 | 6 1 21 12 20 |

Preteen – Teen
Bag of Secrets

MODALITY: Group

GOALS: To clarify role of secrecy in sexual abuse; to help group members understand how offenders manipulate trust and feelings of helplessness

MATERIALS

➤ Worksheet: Clues *following*

➤ Paper and pencils

➤ Worksheet: "Secrets" *following*

➤ Bag labeled with "Top Secret and Confidential"

➤ A bag of gummy worms

METHOD

ADVANCE PREPARATION:
Assemble the materials and make copies of the "Clues" and "Secrets" worksheets.

The group leader explains that there are four clues to the group activity topic. The leader gives each group member a blank piece of paper on which to write a guess. The leader shows the "Clues" sheet to the group members and makes the following statements:

Clue I   "The cat's out of the bag."
Clue II   "There's a skeleton in the closet."
Clue III "I've spilled the beans."
Clue IV   "I've opened a can of worms."

All group members are then asked to write down their guesses as to what those expressions mean. Group members are invited to contribute other expressions for telling and keeping secrets, and a brief discussion is held about the role of secrecy in sexual abuse.

The second part of this activity involves a "Bag of Secrets." Place the bag in the center of the table. Group members answer items on the "Secrets" worksheet one at a time. (Easiest way is to cut them separately and give them out one at a time.) Another way to do this is to give the members blank strips of paper and have the leader read the items.

For example: I kept the secret about sexual abuse for _____
_____
_____

As each item is completed, group members fold the pieces of paper and place them in the "Bag of Secrets." Members take turns reading the responses.

At the end of the activity, the leader says, "I've opened up a can of worms," and each child takes a handful of candy gummy worms.

DISCUSSION

This activity is a fun and easy way to identify commonalities and differences among group members. When permission is given to be anonymous (disguise handwriting or not to sign one's name) a sense of increased safety is created. There is ample opportunity during this activity to discuss privacy vs. secrecy, surprises vs. secrets, and safe secrets vs. unsafe secrets!

As each question is being answered, the children can share their ideas of why the touching took place when no one was around. They may also express feelings about keeping the secret and giving the secret up.

CLUES SHEET

I.

II.

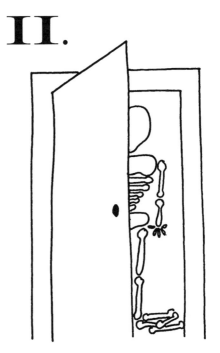

III.

IV

SECRETS WORKSHEET

I kept the secret about sexual abuse for _____

_____

....

The one person I trust with my secrets is _____

_____

....

A secret that I liked to keep was _____

_____

....

The offender made me keep the secret by _____

_____

....

When you have a secret that shouldn't be kept, you could_____

_____

....

If you had a friend who made you promise not to tell he was being sexually abused, you could_____

_____

....

A good secret is_____

_____

....

A secret you shouldn't keep is _____

_____

....

A secret place I'd like to share with a trusted friend is _____

_____

....

Offenders tell kids to keep the secret because _____

_____

....

The hardest part of keeping the sexual abuse a secret was _____

_____

....

Once the secret was out, I felt_____

_____

....

The person I told was _____

_____

....

I picked that person because _____

_____

....

Preteen – Teen
Diary Snoop

MODALITY: Group

GOAL: To help victims understand the elements of secrecy involved in child sexual abuse

MATERIALS

➤ Booklet: "My Diary" (one for each group member) *following*

METHOD

ADVANCE PREPARATION:
The therapist makes 3-page diaries for each group member (cover page, "Dear diary" sentence completion, and blank response page).

ACTIVITY:
The therapist provides each participant with a diary. Group members work individually by filling in the sentence completion. The diaries are then randomly distributed among the group members, so that each group member has a diary belonging to someone else. Group members are told to pretend that they have found the diary belonging to a friend. They are to write a response, giving their friend advice on how to deal with the situation.

DISCUSSION

This age-group will be able to relate well to this activity, because they typically use diary or journal writing to express their feelings and to confide their inner thoughts. The diary exchange provides emotional distance by allowing group members to problem-solve for others rather than to focus on their own personal dilemmas.

BOOKLET

MY
DIARY

Dear Diary:

I have a big secret that I can't tell anyone about. I have been sexually abused! I feel so confused, I don't know what to do. I can't tell anyone about it because

_____

_____

_____

_____

Keeping a secret like this makes me feel _____

_____

_____

_____

I wish I could tell _____ about the sexual abuse, but if I tell, I worry that _____

_____

_____

_____

_____

It feels so weird to have this secret inside— it makes me feel so different. I wish that I could just be like everybody else. I've been thinking about what to do about this for a while, but I haven't come up with any answers. I really need some advice.

Well, bye for now.

Dear _____.

I know I wasn't supposed to snoop around in your diary, but I'm glad I read it because I have some advice to give you. Your situation is really tough, but I think it would help if you _____
_____
_____
_____

If that doesn't work you could try to _____
_____
_____

I also want to tell you that _____
_____
_____
_____

I hope this helps you.

Sincerely,

_____

P.S._____
_____
_____
_____

Chapter 6
Post-Disclosure Experiences

PURPOSE OF THE CHAPTER:

Response to disclosure is a key variable in assessing degree of traumatization. Support systems response, both informal (family) and formal (community), can either facilitate recovery or further add to a child's traumatization. Understanding what happened post-disclosure from the child's point of view will assist in determining if the disclosure process and the post-disclosure response was helpful or harmful to the victim.

The activities in this chapter are divided into two categories:
- Post-disclosure experiences
- Re-framing the disclosure experience as an act of bravery.

Obviously, the first category of activities should precede the second category. The second category of activities are not recommended for use with children who have not disclosed the sexual abuse or whose disclosures were accidental, as these children will feel guilty for not having told. The approach with children who have disclosed accidentally, then, is different. Focus is on their experience, once the validation process has occurred. For children who did not purposely disclose, the leaders may have to process the child's feelings regarding the disclosure process.

This consideration is also true for children who have never disclosed, but were reported for investigation because of a suspicion of abuse and then validated. If, for example, the leaders have a group of children for whom all three circumstances are true (purposeful, accidental, suspicion-reported), it would be important to emphasize their commonalty — each child was experiencing a situation that was unsafe and/or harmful. While it is important to process how children felt about these differences (What do they wish would have happened instead?), focus should be on what happened, not on how it was identified.

On an individual treatment basis, it is important to comprehend how the disclosure process occurred, in order to understand the child's perception of the support available and the child's ability to ask for help. The disclosure experience leading to validation may not have been the child's only attempt to let someone know what was happening. This is also important to assess with children in all three circumstances. The accidental disclosure may have been preceded by one or more attempts to tell, however unsuccessful. How the child perceives these "failed" attempts may impact on the ability to seek help in the future.

Therapists should note the importance of helping the non-offending parent understand the rationale for re-framing the disclosure as an act of bravery. Depending on the experience of the parent, he/she may not be open to viewing the disclosure as a positive act. Parental involvement (from supportive parents) is always an asset; for preschoolers, it is a necessity. If a preschool child does not have a supportive ally, participation in group should be carefully assessed and reconsidered.

Latency — Preteen
Changes Since I told

MODALITY: Individual, group

GOAL: To assess the child's post-disclosure experiences and to normalize feelings of ambivalence regarding disclosure

MATERIALS

➤ Worksheet: "Changes Since I Told" *following*

METHOD

ADVANCE PREPARATION:
Make a copy of the worksheet for each child in the group.

ACTIVITY:
Children complete the worksheet by writing about the changes that have occurred since disclosure at home and at school. They also express how they feel. They write positive changes in the left column under the happy face. Negative changes are written in the right column under the sad face.

The therapist may wish to give the children an example, such as: "A positive change at school since you told may be that you can now concentrate better on your work. A negative change at school may be that kids found out about what happened and are teasing you."

DISCUSSION

Many children often have feelings of regret for having told about the sexual abuse, particularly if they were re-victimized during the disclosure and post-disclosure phase. This activity provides children with a forum to process their positive, negative, or ambivalent feelings about disclosure.

This activity was developed for the Crisis Support Group Program at the Metropolitan Toronto Special Committee on Child Abuse and is being used with permission.

WORKSHEET

CHANGES SINCE I TOLD

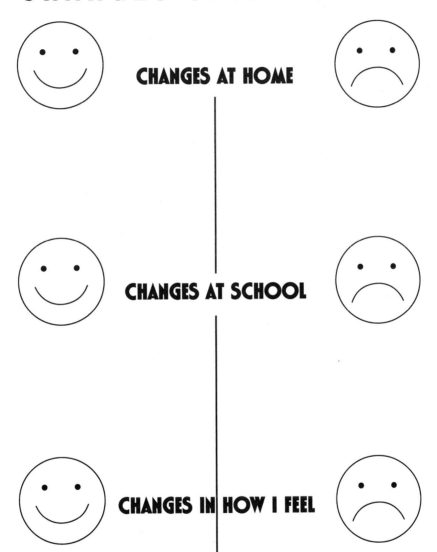

CHANGES AT HOME

CHANGES AT SCHOOL

CHANGES IN HOW I FEEL

Latency — Teen
Before & After

MODALITY: Individual, group

GOALS: To assess the victim's perceptions of what has changed since the disclosure of sexual abuse; to assess the child's emotional belief system regarding responsibility for family upheaval; to assess the degree of stress experienced by the child as a result of disclosure

MATERIALS

➤ Worksheet: "Before I Told" *following*

➤ Worksheet: "After I Told" *following*

➤ Pencils

METHOD

ADVANCE PREPARATION:
Make copies of the two worksheets for each group member. Make sure pencils are available.

ACTIVITY:
An interesting way to introduce this activity is to select a variety of "before and after" articles from fashion magazines and distribute them to group members. Many of these are available in magazines. The most popular ones focus on makeup, hairstyles, and weight loss.

The group discusses "changes"—and how some changes are for better, some for worse. The leader then guides the discussion to changes since disclosure. Each group member receives a "Before I Told" and After I Told" checklist, which is completed individually. The leader might read aloud the items as members complete the checklist. This keeps members focused on the task. It also eliminates any embarrassment that might occur for poor readers or difficulties that children whose first language is not English might have.

DISCUSSION

This activity can be used as a diagnostic tool to assess areas of traumatization for the victim. More specifically, the activity assesses the victim's perspective of responsibility in the sexual abuse, response to disclosure, feelings associated with the disclosure, the victim's relationship with significant others, the victim's coping strategies.

NOTE: As each checklist is quite lengthy, the therapist may wish to divide the activity over two sessions.

WORKSHEET

BEFORE I TOLD

- ☐ I thought nobody would believe me.
- ☐ I thought I would be put in a foster home.
- ☐ I thought my parent(s) would kill the abuser.
- ☐ I thought people would be mad at me.
- ☐ I thought my family would break up.
- ☐ I thought the abuser would hurt me or someone I cared for.
- ☐ I thought I would be punished if I told.
- ☐ I thought I would be believed.
- ☐ I thought the abuse would stop.
- ☐ I thought I would never have to talk about what happened.
- ☐ I thought the abuser would admit what he did.
- ☐ I thought the abuser would cry.
- ☐ I thought that people would understand.
- ☐ I thought my family would be ashamed of me.
- ☐ I thought that people would believe the abuser.
- ☐ I thought we would have to move.
- ☐ I thought my mother would tell everybody in the family.
- ☐ I thought my friends would find out and ask me embarrassing questions.
- ☐ I thought things like this only happened to bad kids.
- ☐ I thought they would put the abuser in jail right away.

- ☐ I thought my mother would feel sorry for the abuser.
- ☐ I thought my family would turn against me.
- ☐ I thought my family would turn against the abuser.
- ☐ I thought the abuser would lie about what had happened.
- ☐ I thought I was the only one this kind of thing happened to.
- ☐ I thought the abuser wouldn't love me if I told.
- ☐ I thought the abuser would start abusing someone else.
- ☐ I thought sex was something private I shouldn't talk about.
- ☐ I thought nobody could do anything to help me.
- ☐ I thought I would get help.

WORKSHEET

AFTER I TOLD

- ☐ When the secret came out, the person I told believed me.
- ☐ I was embarrassed when I talked to the police and the social worker.
- ☐ I was afraid that the abuser would hurt me.
- ☐ I was afraid that no one would understand.
- ☐ I was worried that the abuser would stop loving me because I told what happened.
- ☐ I felt like it was my fault that the abuse happened.
- ☐ I missed the abuser.
- ☐ I felt that people in my family would feel sorry for the abuser.
- ☐ Kids at school made fun of me.
- ☐ People asked me questions I didn't want to answer.
- ☐ People believed I was brave to tell.
- ☐ The abuser admitted what he did to me.
- ☐ The abuser lied about what happened.
- ☐ My parents seemed upset because I told about what happened.
- ☐ My parents blamed each other for what happened to me.
- ☐ Not everybody in my family knew what happened to me.
- ☐ I had no control over what happened to me.
- ☐ People listened to me when I talked about what happened to me.
- ☐ I was allowed to get away with anything I want.
- ☐ I had bad moods.
- ☐ I felt like running away.
- ☐ I worried about going to court.

- ☐ It seemed that my parents wouldn't let me have any freedom.
- ☐ My parents fought more when the secret came out.
- ☐ I felt like the problem got worse since I told.
- ☐ When my mother found out about the abuse she cried a lot.
- ☐ I had bad dreams since the secret came out.
- ☐ I couldn't concentrate on my school work.
- ☐ Lots of things remind me of the abuse.
- ☐ I'd just like to forget about what happened.
- ☐ None of my brothers or sisters can see the offender.
- ☐ I feel like hurting myself.
- ☐ Nothing changed.
- ☐ I didn't tell everything.
- ☐ I feel I'm abnormal because I have a lot of sexual thoughts.
- ☐ I'm worried I might become a sexual abuser.
- ☐ After I told, I had to go live in a foster home/group home.
- ☐ I got in trouble after I told.
- ☐ I felt embarrassed that my family told people about what happened.
- ☐ I'm getting help.
- ☐ The abuse stopped.

Latency – Teen
My Story

MODALITY: Individual, group

GOALS: To assess the child's experience of disclosure; to normalize fears about the telling process; to acknowledge the family turmoil resulting from the disclosure process; to affirm the victim's bravery for having told the secret

MATERIALS

➤ Workbook: "My Story" (two versions—for younger and older clients) *following*

➤ Pencils

➤ Bravery buttons (for younger children); certificates (for older children)

METHOD

ADVANCE PREPARATION:
Make copies of the workbook and bravery buttons for each child. Place pencils within reach of the children.

ACTIVITY:
Each child completes the "My Story" Workbook. The workbook asks children various questions concerning disclosure-related information.

The workbooks can help children discuss what happens when the secret of sexual abuse is revealed. Children are encouraged to share their experiences and to identify commonalties as well as differences. Once the workbook is completed, therapists award the younger children with "Bravery Buttons" and the older children with certificates.

DISCUSSION

This workbook elicits valuable information related to how the victim was responded to at the time of disclosure. The activity also helps children to explore and express their feelings related to the disclosure.

Some children may feel happy and relieved, particularly if they were believed and supported at the time of disclosure. Other children will feel guilty if they were made to feel responsible for not having told sooner, disrupting the family, or getting the abuser in trouble. Children may also feel scared if they fear the abuser will harm them or a family member. If the child was removed from the home following the disclosure, there may be feelings of rejection, anger, sadness, etc.

The workbook can help children process their feelings. The child is provided with a sense of support and empowerment by affirming that the disclosure was an act of bravery.

* This activity was developed for the Crisis Support Group Program at the Metropolitan Toronto Special Committee on Child Abuse and is being used with their permission.

WORKBOOK

MY STORY

My name is:_____

I am _____ years old.

I was sexually abused by: _____

I kept the secret about being sexually abused for: _____ (days/months/years).

I kept the abuse a secret because I worried that:

_____

_____

_____

_____

The first person I told about the sexual abuse was:

_____

When I told about the sexual abuse, this is what happened: (Check all that happened.)

☐ I was believed.

☐ I was not believed.

☐ I had to talk to a social worker.

☐ I had to talk to the police.

☐ The abuser got in trouble.

☐ I got in trouble.

☐ Things at home got better.

☐ Things at home got worse.

(Fill in the face to show how you feel.)
Now I feel:

(Fill in the face to show how the abuser feels.)
The abuser feels:

(Fill in the faces to show how they feel.)
My family feels:

These are the people who know I am not to blame for what happened:

_____

_____

_____

(Unscramble the word below.)
Because I told about the abuse I am:

AVEBR

__ __ __ __ __ !

BRAVERY BUTTON

To make a bravery button, cut out the circles below, trace the circle onto cardboard or colored bristol board, and paste together. Cut out the button. Use a safety pin to attach the button onto the client.

MY STORY

Before people found out I was being sexually abused I felt _____

_____

I kept the sexual abuse a secret because I worried that

_____

I decided to tell because _____

_____

I thought after I told about the abuse _____

_____

But what really happened when I told was _____

_____

What I would have liked _____ to say to me when I told
about the abuse was _____

_____

What _____ really said to me was _____

_____

Now I feel _____, and I think the

abuser feels _____, and my mom feels _____

_____, and my _____ feels

_____ .

'I Did It Myself'
Award

On _____, a crime was reported.
The crime was sexual abuse and the victim was _____

This certificate is presented in honor of
the bravery
that this act of courage required.

Children are protected by the law and are never
responsible in any way for sexual abuse.

Latency – Teen
Dear Group

MODALITY: Individual, group

GOAL: To validate feelings of turmoil and family upheaval resulting from disclosure; to assess resources and support for victims

MATERIALS

➤ Letter: "Dear Group" *following*

➤ Pens/pencils

➤ Paper

➤ Flip chart and markers

METHOD

ADVANCE PREPARATION:
Provide paper for children to use to write their letters. Make pencils or pens available. Use a flip chart and markers if a letter will be written as a group activity.

ACTIVITY:
The leader begins by explaining that the purpose of the activity is to help group members talk about problems that have occurred since the secret came out. Victims should be encouraged to share the

experiences that have happened to them. In introducing the letter, the group leader says, "The letter represents experiences and feelings from more than one victim. Some of the things that happened to the writer may be similar to your situation. Other parts may be quite different."

The leader reads to the group, and members are invited to respond in writing. The responses may be written individually or as a group.

The second part of this activity is to have group members write a letter that tells what happened when they told the secret. They can write to an advice expert such as Dear Abby or to a friend or trusted adult. Letters can be written to the group as well.

After the letters have been written, they may be read aloud to the group and exchanged for advice.

DISCUSSION

The therapeutic value of sharing the positive and negative changes since disclosure is important. Acknowledgement that all change is scary because of the unknown can be emphasized. Relationships that have been damaged need to be acknowledged and mourned.

As the children share their own feelings and experiences, they will gain support from other group members. This helps dissolve some feelings of isolation and abandonment.

SAMPLE LETTER TO THE GROUP

Dear Group,

    I have a big problem. Ever since I told my teacher that my step-brother was sexually abusing me, things have gotten really bad for me. All I wanted was for him to stop. What happened after was terrible. My mom has been crying her eyes out all the time when she thinks I don't see her. She got really mad that I hadn't told about it right away and that I told my teacher. She and my step-dad are fighting — screaming at each other. My step-dad has moved out with my step-brother. This has really busted up my family. In spite of everything other people say, I feel that telling about the abuse was a big mistake.

Preschool
Brave Little Bears

MODALITY: Individual, group

GOALS: To assess the child's post-disclosure experiences; to affirm the child's bravery for having disclosed the sexual abuse; to normalize fears about the telling process

MATERIALS

➤ Scenarios: "Brave Little Bears" *following*

➤ Paper (typewriter paper size)

➤ Bear outline *following*

➤ Scissors

➤ Black marker

➤ Star stickers (4 per child)

➤ Yellow construction paper

➤ Safety pins

METHOD

ADVANCE PREPARATION:

To make a string of four paper bears, fold one piece of paper from end to end in half, then fold it in half again. Cut out the attached outline of the bear and place it on the folded paper so that the end of the hands are touching the left and right folds. Trace the bear onto the folded paper. Cut out the bear, making sure not to cut the ends of the hands where the folds are. Gently open the string of paper bears. Draw a face on each bear using a black marker. Cut the yellow construction paper into stars—one for each child.

ACTIVITY:

Provide each child with a string of four paper bears and four self-adhesive star stickers. The therapist selects four of the seven "Brave Little Bear" scenarios from the attached sheet. The therapist states that she is going to read a story about a brave little bear. The first scenario is read aloud to the children. Each child then takes turns saying who they told about the sexual abuse. Once a child has given a response, the child sticks a star onto one of the paper bears. Each child should be given an opportunity to respond to the question and to place a star sticker on one of the four paper bears before the therapist moves on to the next round.

When all the children have had a turn for the first round, the therapist reads the next scenario and the children answer the question and put a star on another paper bear. This continues until all four scenarios have been read and the children have answered the four questions. At the end of this activity, the therapist states, "You are all very brave just like the brave little bear. You each deserve a star for your bravery!" Each child is awarded a paper star to wear.

Another way to close this activity is to gather the children for a "Teddy Bear Picnic" and award the children at the picnic with a star for bravery, as well as teddy bear related items, such as teddy stickers and gummy bears. Poems from the book *Bear Hugs* (Kathleen Hague, New York: Henry Holt and Company, 1989) can be read aloud to the children at the Teddy Bear Picnic .

DISCUSSION

Victims who receive support and validation for their disclosure of sexual abuse have a better chance for recovery. Through this activity, children will feel a sense of support and empowerment as their bravery is proclaimed. *This activity is not recommended for use with children who have not disclosed the sexual abuse or whose disclosures were accidental, because these children will feel guilty for not having told.*

SCENARIOS:
BRAVE LITTLE BEARS

1) One little bear had a secret. It wasn't a fun, safe secret like when his parents bought him a big jar of honey for his birthday. It was a bad, scary secret about somebody who had touched his private parts and told him not to tell. But he was a brave little bear and he told his parents about the secret touching trouble. This little bear did the right thing. He was a brave little bear!

Who did you tell about the secret touching?

2) This little bear had to talk to the police about the secret touching. The police officer asked the little bear lots of questions about exactly what happened. The little bear was scared but he told the police officer all about the secret touching. The police officer told the little bear that he did nothing wrong. The person who touched the little bear's private parts knew he was doing something wrong and he was to blame. The police officer told the little bear that he was very brave for telling.

Did you talk to the police about the secret touching?

3) Sometimes at night when the little bear was sleeping, he had bad dreams. He would wake up feeling very scared. But then he remembered to tell himself that he was a brave little bear and this made him feel much better.

Tell about a scary dream you had.

4) The little bear had to go to court to tell the judge about the secret touching. He was very scared. But then he remembered

that all he had to do was to tell the truth about the secret touching. This made him feel better. He went into the court room feeling brave because he was a brave little bear!

What was it like when you went to court?

5) The little bear had to go to the doctor. The doctor had to check the little bear's private parts to make sure he was OK. The little bear was scared, but his mom came into the room with him and held his paw as the doctor checked him. This made the little bear feel much better. The doctor told the little bear that he was very brave!

What was it like when you went to the doctor?

6) After the little bear told about the secret touching, he had to go live in a foster home. He got very homesick and he missed his mommy. He thought he was put in the foster home because he was bad. But then the foster mother told him that he was in the foster home to make sure that he was safe and that nobody would hurt him again. The foster mother told the little bear the he was very brave for telling about the secret touching and that he did nothing wrong. This made the little bear feel much better.

How did you feel when you first went to live in the foster home?

7) The little bear went to a group where there were other little bears who had been touched on their private parts and been told to keep it a secret. All the bears in the group were very brave because they had told somebody about the secret touching. At first the little bear was scared and nervous having to talk to the other bears in the group. But then he remembered he was a brave little bear, so when it came to his turn he took a deep breath and said his name out loud.

How did you feel when you first came to this group?

BEAR OUTLINE

Latency – Preteen
Kid Hero

MODALITY: Individual, group

GOAL: To reframe the disclosure of sexual abuse as an act of bravery

MATERIALS

➤ Newspaper Booklet (one per child) *following*

➤ Picture of each child (or magazine picture to represent the child)

METHOD

ADVANCE PREPARATION:
Make copies of the newspaper booklet to distribute to each group member. Collect magazine pictures of children.

ACTIVITY:
Each child completes a copy of "The Daily News." The booklet has various activities focused on affirming the child's bravery for having disclosed the sexual abuse. Once completed, the booklets can be redistributed among the group for others to read. If the child wishes, the completed newspaper can be photocopied and "delivered" to people, such as to the child's non-offending parent.

DISCUSSION

This activity provides children with a sense of empowerment and support for having told about the abuse. It is therefore a particularly helpful activity for children who lack support and validation regarding their disclosure.

NEWSPAPER BOOKLET
DAILY NEWS 1

The Daily News

Kid Hero!

[Draw a picture of yourself or paste a picture of yourself here.]

My Story
Why I Told About the Sexual Abuse
by _____

_____

_____

_____

_____

_____

_____

_____

DAILY NEWS 2

TIPS FOR PARENTS AND OTHER GROWN-UPS WHO LOVE KIDS WHO HAVE BEEN SEXUALLY ABUSED.

WHY KIDS WHO TELL ABOUT SEXUAL ABUSE ARE BRAVE!

1.

1.

2.

2.

3.

3.

4.

4.

5.

5.

6.

6.

7.

7.

8.

8.

9.

9.

<u>DAILY NEWS 3</u>

IT HAPPENS TO LOTS OF PEOPLE

INTERVIEW WITH LINDA

Linda is a grown-up who was seually abused when she was a kid. Interviewed just before group, she stated:

"When I was a little girl, I was sexually abused, too. I didn't have a chance to attend a therapy group. You kids are lucky to have a chance to share your feelings with other kids who are going through some of the same things."

Hang in there heroes!

WRITE A QUESTION FOR LINDA

_____

_____

_____

_____

_____

_____

_____

CONTEST

Win Prizes!

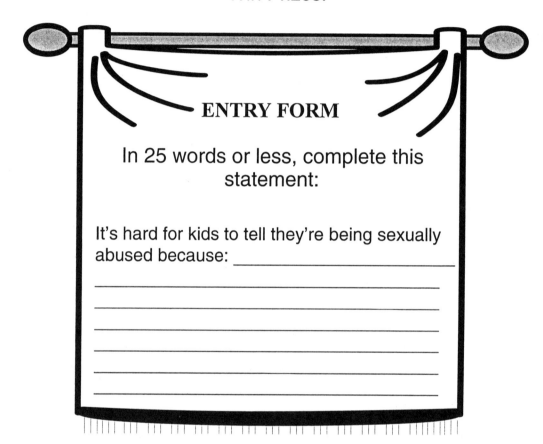

ENTRY FORM

In 25 words or less, complete this statement:

It's hard for kids to tell they're being sexually abused because: _____
_____
_____
_____
_____
_____
_____

Hey Kids !!
Need to Talk?

• Free
• Confidential
• The Kids' Help Phone number is:

_____

All Ages
Disclosure Day

MODALITY: Group

GOALS: To reframe the upheaval associated with the disclosure of sexual abuse into an act to be honored and commemorated; to affirm the courage required to disclose abuse

Note: This activity has three parts; each part structured for a separate age-group.

For School-Aged Children

MATERIALS

➤ Certificates: "Disclosure Day" *following*

➤ Worksheet: "Disclosure Day" *following*

➤ Plastic bags for loot bags

➤ Dice

➤ Assortment of party decorations

➤ Plastic champagne glasses

➤ Ginger ale or sparkling grape juice

➤ 6 suggested party favors

➤ Stars (stickers or confetti)

➤ Band-Aids

➤ Balloons

➤ Noisemakers or party horns

➤ Heart stickers

➤ Artificial flowers

METHOD

ADVANCE PREPARATION:
Copy the certificate and worksheet to use with the children. Collect the other items to use for the celebration.

ACTIVITY:
Each player first completes a "DISCLOSURE DAY" worksheet. When all members have filled in their sheets, the therapist leads a discussion, inviting group members to share their experiences of the day on which they disclosed their sexual abuse. Many of the memories would include feelings of embarrassment, and fear, as well as unpleasant occurences. The therapist then asks group members to think of each person's bravery and the courage required to disclose sexual abuse.

The leader has group members brainstorm a list of special events and holidays which they already celebrate. The group can share ways in which they honor people such as singing songs, having parties, sending cards, giving presents, etc.

The leader then explains that the group is going to celebrate their bravery by playing the "Celebrate Disclosure Game." Each of the six boxes is assigned a number to correspond with the numbers on the die. Players take turns rolling the die and reading questions which match the die numbers, such as if a player rolls 4, the question is: "What really did happen?" All players then share their answers in Box 4. At the end of each question, a party favor is awarded for children to place in their loot bags. Affirmations are declared as follows.

Box # 1   Have a heart, it shows your strength!

Box # 2   Take a star to represent how brave you were to tell.

Box # 3   Blow your horn! Show how proud you should be for telling about the sexual abuse.

Box # 4   Sexual Abuse hurts kids.
Take a Band-Aid to represent how hard it was to tell.

Box # 5   Help yourself to a balloon. It celebrates your courage.

Box # 6   Award yourself a flower. It shows how precious you are and how you will blossom into a wonderful human being!

The game is played until all six numbers of the dice have been rolled and each of the six questions on the worksheet has been answered. When all questions have been answered and the loot bags filled with party favors, group members can take turns clinking glasses of ginger ale or grape juice to celebrate their own and each other's bravery.

DISCLOSURE DAY WORKSHEET

-1- WHO I TOLD ABOUT THE ABUSE:	-2- WHAT HAPPENED WHEN I TOLD:
-3- WHO BELIEVED AND HELPED ME:	-4- WHO DIDN'T BELIEVE ME:
-5- HOW I FELT WHEN I TOLD:	-6- HOW I FEEL NOW:

'I Did It Myself' Award

On _____, a crime was reported.
The crime was sexual abuse and the victim was _____

This certificate is presented in honor of
the bravery
that this act of courage required.

Children are protected by the law and are never
responsible in any way for sexual abuse.

DISCLOSURE DAY

Once the children have documented details and feelings associated with their disclosure, a party atmosphere helps to reframe their disclosure as an act of courage and bravery.

FOR OLDER CHILDREN AND TEENS

GREETING CARDS

For older children, the "party" atmosphere can be created with a slight modification and will still enable the group to address disclosure as an event to be celebrated. In place of the game, greeting cards can be constructed to commemorate the courage of sexual abuse victims.

MATERIALS

➤ Assorted greeting cards

➤ Assorted greeting card messages *following*

➤ Markers

➤ Stickers

➤ Glitter

➤ Scissors

METHOD

ADVANCE PREPARATION:
Bring in an assortment of greeting cards. Make enough copies of each greeting card message to use in this activity.

ACTIVITY:
The activity begins with the group examining the various greeting cards. Be sure to include sympathy and get well cards in the assortment because they will make the point that some events which are commemorated are not purely joyful. These will allow you to lead

easily into the discussion of how one could celebrate a victim's bravery and courage in disclosing sexual abuse.

The therapist then provides the greeting card messages, and group members send cards to each other and themselves.

Dear _____,

What happened to you was
really rotten. I'm sorry you're
going through all the upset.
Hang in there!

FOLD

‒ CUT

Dear _____,

You were brave to tell about
what happened to you.

Dear _____,

Congratulations for telling what happened to you. You were a trusting child and you should never have been sexually abused.

CUT

FOLD

Dear _____,

You are not to blame for what happened. You did not know how to say "NO." You were tricked into keeping the secret.

Dear _____,

Telling about sexual abuse is hard. It's a time of confusing feelings. I'm thinking about you and wishing you well.

FOLD

- CUT

Dear _____,

You are not to blame for what happened. You did not know how to say "NO." You were tricked into keeping the secret.

Dear _____,

Hooray for you! You reported a crime.

FOLD

CUT

Dear _____,

You are not responsible because the offender can no longer have contact with you or your family. He knew what he did was against the law.

Dear _____,

Telling about sexual abuse is hard. It's a time of confusing feelings. I'm thinking about you and wishing you well.

FOLD

— CUT

Dear _____,

You are not responsible for your family's breaking up. You did not cause this to happen. The problems happened because the offender sexually abused you.

PAPER DOLLS AND PAPER AIRPLANES

FOR PRESCHOOLERS

PARTY HATS

The activity can be easily modified for very young children.

MATERIALS:

- ➤ Ribbons
- ➤ Glitter
- ➤ Scraps for decorating
- ➤ String

- ➤ Glue sticks
- ➤ Pencils
- ➤ Scissors
- ➤ Thin colored cardboard

METHOD

ADVANCE PREPARATION:

Make a party hat for each group member by rolling a piece of paper into the shape of a cone, taping it together, and placing string on two sides to tie it once it is on the child's head.

ACTIVITY:

The leader facilitates a group discussion about how brave the children are because they told about the secret touching. The hats are intorduced as a way for the children to celebrate their bravery. The children can decorate the hats in any way they wish. The leader can add words like *BRAVE, TERRIFIC, WOW* to commend their bravery.

The leader can encourage the children to celebrate their own and other kids' bravery for telling about the abuse. Parents and care givers are asked to toast the children and sing party songs.

(Sing to the tune of "Happy Birthday")
>Happy Brave Day to You
>Happy Brave Day to You
>You found such great courage
>and we're proud of you too.
>A N D
>It's OK to say no
>It's OK to say no
>When someone you don't want touches you
>It's OK to say no.

DISCUSSION

This activity can be remarkably therapeutic in helping children alter their view of disclosure of sexual abuse. The upheaval which results from a sexual abuse investigation very often is traumatic for the victims. It is not uncommon for children to wish that they had never disclosed the sexual abuse. Many victims regret ever having broken silence. Anything that celebrates their bravery and honors their courage is helpful for their recovery.

Care must be taken to honor the feelings of victims who can't find any positive aspect of disclosing. One member proposed a toast to a fellow group member: "I hope one day you will know how really brave you are – even though you can't right now."

The reader should note that it is important to clarify for the group members exactly what is being celebrated in this activity. For instance, the therapist can say to the group: "We are not celebrating the fact that you were sexually abused. We are not celebrating the fact that the abuser may have gone to jail. What we are celebrating is how brave each of you are because we know how hard it was to tell about the sexual abuse."

Note: This activity is not recommended for use with children who did not disclose the sexual abuse, as this activity will reinforce any feelings of guilt for not having told.

Chapter 7
Documenting the Sexual Abuse

PURPOSE OF THE CHAPTER:
Grounding trauma (externalizing the event in a concrete and observable way) is an essential element in the healing process. The authors have separated this process from "disclosure experiences" in an attempt to differentiate disclosing from actually documenting.

The activities in this chapter serve to facilitate "processing to a product" (Hindman, 1991) and enable children to have a lasting, accurate record of what happened to them. This activity assists the child in bringing closure to experiences in order to continue with healthy development. In addition to the activities described in this chapter, many more activities can be developed, such as journaling, to further process externalization.

Preschool – Latency
Go Fish

MODALITY: Group

GOALS: To encourage children to disclose information about the sexual abuse using a less threatening modality; to provide support and positive reinforcement for self-disclosing; to decrease feelings of isolation by allowing children to share information about the abuse with others in like circumstances

MATERIALS

➤ Worksheet: "Go Fish" *following*

➤ Cardboard

➤ Fish outline *following*

➤ Stick or hanger

➤ String

➤ Paper clip

➤ Magnet

➤ Fish pond (small child's wading pool, laundry basket or decorated box)

➤ Fish stickers (one per player)

➤ Pennies (one per player)

➤ 2 bags

METHOD

ADVANCE PREPARATION:
Make copies of the worksheet. Trace the fish patterns onto the cardboard. Cut out the fish patterns. Repeat this so there are 11 cardboard fish. Label five of the fish with: *Answer a question.* Label another three fish with: *Do something fun and silly!* Label the remaining fish with: *Pick a surprise!*

Label one bag *Do Something Fun and Silly.* Label the other bag *Pick a Surprise.*

Attach a paper clip onto each fish. Dump the fish into the fish pond. To make a fishing pole, tie a string to the stick. Tie a magnet onto the end of the string.

Cut out three pieces of paper and write a *fun and silly* instruction on each one, such as: "Try to touch your nose with your tongue"; "Quack like a duck"; "Walk backwards from one end of the room to the other." Place these in the bag labeled *Fun and Silly.*

Cut out another three pieces of paper and write a *pick a surprise* instruction on each one, such as: "Freddy, the fish, says you are very brave! Take a fish sticker and give one to each player"; "You deserve a hug! Pick someone in the group to give you a hug"; "Take a lucky penny and give one to each player. Take turns making a wish and throwing your penny in the pond!" Place these in the bag labeled *Pick a Surprise.*

ACTIVITY:
For the first part of the activity, each child completes the "Go Fish" worksheets. Each child should complete the worksheet with the assistance of an adult helper (care giver or group leader). Children can answer each question verbally and the adult helper can write the responses inside the fish on the worksheet. The children's responses

should be written verbatim. Children should not be forced to give an answer to questions they are not yet ready to answer.

Once the children have completed their worksheets, they sit in a circle with the fish pond placed in the middle. One child is chosen to go first. The child uses the fishing pole to "catch a fish" (hook a magnet to a fish in the pond). If the child catches a fish labeled *Answer a Question*, the child shares the response from the first question on the worksheet. The other players then have an opportunity to answer the same question. (In order to respect each child's readiness to share details of the abuse, the leader can make a rule that players share what they wish with the group.)

If a child catches a fish labeled *Do Something Fun and Silly,* then the child chooses an instruction from the bag labeled *Fun and Silly*.

If the child catches a fish labeled *Pick a Surprise* then he or she chooses an instruction from the bag with the same label. The game continues until all the fish have been caught.

DISCUSSION

This activity provides a non-threatening way for children to share what happened to them. The therapist should ensure that children do not feel coerced into sharing details of the abuse. The game format coupled with the mutual support of the group generally encourages open communication among the children.

It may be helpful to meet with the care givers prior to the group session to prepare them for how they can best support their children during the activity.   They can be shown the worksheet ahead of time so they know what kind of questions to expect. Care givers can be prompted to give supportive messages to their children, such as "You can tell me anything—I will always love you and take care of you!"

WORKSHEET: GO FISH

Who sexually abused you?
(Who touched your private parts?)

What do you remember about
when the secret touching
happened?

How did you feel when the secret
touching was happening?

How do you feel now when you
think about the secret touching?

What would you say to other kids who
had secret touching happen to them?

FISH OUTLINE

Latency—Preteen
Hunt for Buried Treasure

MODALITY: Individual, group

GOALS: To encourage children to disclose information about the sexual abuse, using a less threatening modality; to provide support and positive reinforcement for self-disclosing; and to decrease feelings of isolation by allowing the children to share information about the sexual abuse with others in like circumstances

MATERIALS

➤ Worksheet: Treasure Map *following*

➤ Box

➤ Newspaper or confetti

➤ Small gift boxes (one per child)

➤ "Congratulations" Cards

➤ Wrapping paper

➤ Stickers (stars, teddy bears, happy faces)

➤ Hershey's Kisses

➤ One die

➤ Key to Buried Treasure *following*

➤ Bag

➤ Clear tape to assemble the puzzle

M E T H O D

ADVANCE PREPARATION:

The therapist fills each gift box with one Hershey's Kiss and stickers (one star, one teddy bear, and one happy face). A card is placed in each box which says, "Congratulations on reaching the buried treasure! You have been very brave on this journey and you are being rewarded with some special gifts: a star for your bravery, a teddy bear for a bear hug, a happy face for getting the secret out, and a Hershey's Kiss because we care about you!"

The gift boxes are then wrapped separately and placed in a decorated "BURIED TREASURE" box. The box (or treasure chest) is filled with shredded newspaper or confetti to bury the gift boxes. If desired, the gift boxes can be buried in the box under stones that have been painted gold.

The key to the buried treasure can be copied onto yellow or gold cardboard paper, and cut into enough pieces so that each group member gets a piece of the puzzle during the activity. The pieces of the key puzzle are placed in a bag.

The Treasure Map should be enlarged on a photocopy machine or copied onto larger butcher's paper so that children have ample room to write their responses. Each child should be provided with their own treasure map.

ACTIVITY:

The therapist provides each child with a treasure map. The children are told the following: "You are going on a hunt for buried treasure. To get to the treasure, answer each question on the treasure map. This is *not* a contest to see who can finish first, so take your time on this journey."

The children then complete their treasure maps by filling in the answers to each of the questions.

Once the children have completed their maps, they can share their responses with the group. In order to respect each child's readiness to share details of the abuse, the group leader can make a rule that group members may share what they wish with the group. After each child shares his or her worksheet with the group, the child takes a piece of the key puzzle from the bag. Once all group members have finished sharing and discussing their activity, each child places his or her piece of the puzzle in the middle of the floor, and the group works together to assemble the puzzle, to form the key to open the treasure chest. Each child then takes a gift box from the treasure chest.

If used in individual therapy, the child can write the answers on the Treasure Map. Once the Treasure Map is completed, the child can reach into the treasure chest to retrieve the buried treasure.

DISCUSSION

Self-disclosing details of the sexual abuse can be anxiety-provoking for children. The Treasure Map provides children with a less threatening way to share their stories. Nevertheless, some children will continue to have difficulty sharing details of their abuse experiences. If this is the case, the therapist can validate the feelings and explore the reasons underlying the child's resistance. The therapist should not overreact as children share details of the sexual abuse. The therapist should take on a neutral, yet supportive role, and should listen to the children rather than telling them how to feel.

The therapist can make this activity more appealing by providing the children with dress-up clothes for their treasure hunt. For instance, children can easily be transformed into pirates by wearing bandanas and eye patches! In addition, the Treasure Map can be singed along the edges to create a more "authentic" map. The treasure chest can be painted gold and filled with gold-foil wrapped chocolate coins and colorful hard candies for jewels.

WORKSHEET

Treasure Map

You are on a hunt for buried treasure. Answer each question on your treasure map to get to the buried treasure.

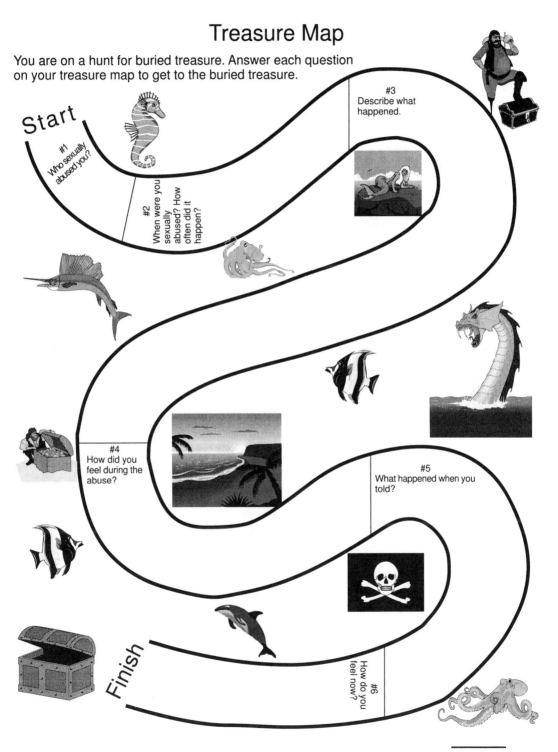

Start

#1
Who sexually abused you?

#2
When were you sexually abused? How often did it happen?

#3
Describe what happened.

#4
How did you feel during the abuse?

#5
What happened when you told?

#6
How do you feel now?

Finish

KEY TO BURIED TREASURE

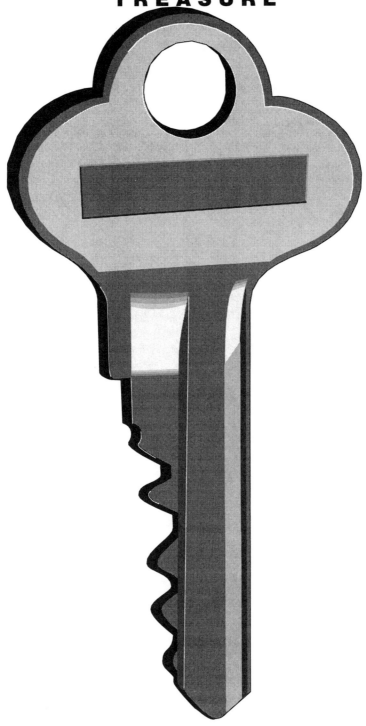

HUNT FOR BURIED TREASURE

This activity is always a hit, especially with active boys. It allows children to deal with a potentially overwhelming subject from a safe and playful distance. Costumes shown here all came from the birthday party supply section of the local discount store. Use your imagination for props!

Preteen – Teen
My Autobiography

MODALITY: Individual, group

GOALS: To encourage self-disclosure; to decrease feelings of isolation by allowing youngsters to share information about their abuse with others in like circumstances; to balance feelings of victimization with feelings of competence

MATERIALS

➤ "Autobiography" Booklet *following*

➤ Blank journals for each group member to take home, or supplies for group members to create home-made journals.

METHOD

ADVANCE PREPARATION:
Make copies of the "Autobiography" pages to use with the children.

ACTIVITY:
In this activity, teens write their autobiographies by completing the sentences in this exercise. Note that these sentences are only a guide, so clients should be encouraged to write their autobiographies as they wish. The therapist should have extra paper and coloring materials available for teens who want to illustrate their

autobiographies. At the end of the activity, group members can be provided with journals to take home with them, or supplies to make their own journals. The group can discuss the therapeutic benefits of creative writing and journaling.

DISCUSSION

Many teens feel overwhelmed by what happened to them. The autobiography provides victims with a structure to tell of their sexual abuse within the context of other important life events.

It is important to help teens relate what happened to them, while at the same time enabling them to recognize that the sexual abuse does not define who they are.

The purpose of this activity is to provide victims with an identity that is not overpowered by the sexual abuse. The therapist can anticipate that group members will have different comfort levels in disclosing details of the sexual abuse. Group members should not feel pressured to self-disclose, and their right to privacy should be respected. The therapist and fellow group members will be instrumental in creating an atmosphere of support and safety so that self-disclosure is encouraged.

BOOKLET

MY AUTOBIOGRAPHY

My name is _____ . I was born in

_____ on the _____ day of _____ in 19___.

One of the most important things that you should know about me as a

little baby is that I _____

_____

_____ .

My family _____ .

_____

When I first started school, I remember that _____

_____ .

An important memory I have about my grade school years is when

_____ .

I remember really enjoying_____

and laughing about _____ .

I remember a favorite holiday was _____ because_____

_____ .

One of the things I was really good at was _____

_____ .

When I was _____ I was sexually abused by _____ .

I remember the first time it happened. The abuser said_____

_____

and I responded by _____

_____ .

The abuser did things to me like _____

and he/she also _____

_____

_____ .

During the sexual abuse I felt _____ .

The abuse went on for _____ . I kept the secret about

being sexually abused for _____ because I was worried that____

_____ .

The first person I told about the sexual abuse was _____ .

When I told, I was surprised that _____

_____ .

Now my family _____ .

If I were to see the abuser, I would _____

_____ .

Although when I think about the abuse I feel_____

there are a lot of things that cheer me up and make me feel better, like

_____ and _____ .

This past year, one of the things I did that I am very proud of is ____

_____ .

This is my life so far, and I hope that in the years ahead _____

_____ .

As you can see, there have been some ups and some downs in my life. There are good memories that I can look back on, and things that I have done that make me feel proud. The sexual abuse is something that should never have happened, because I was an innocent child. Telling about what happened to me is hard, but it is important to help me get better. One last thing I want to say is to all the other kids out there who have been sexually abused: I hope that you _____

_____

_____

_____

_____.

Chapter 8
Responsibility

PURPOSE OF THE CHAPTER:

The issue of responsibility—or self-blame—is complex and multidimensional. The key to assessing self-blame dynamics lies in understanding the individual child's emotional belief system regarding why the sexual abuse occurred. This critical issue is unique to each child. For a young child, going over to a neighbor's house when told not to may constitute a reason for feeling responsible. Accepting gifts, responding to special attention, and any number of possible scenarios may tie the child to the belief that he or she is guilty. While there are many similarities among children and their thinking about responsibility, it is important to stress the need for assessing each child's perception of her or his sense of responsibility for what happened.

In addition to this dimension (i.e., "I did something to cause the sexual abuse"), there are several others which may contribute or reinforce a child's feeling of self-blame. For example, if the child perceives that his or her significant others do not believe in the child's innocence, or that they support the offender overtly or covertly, the child's sense of innocence is undermined.

The activities in this section are designed to provide ways to identify and correct cognitive distortions and externalize confusions which serve to keep the child in a state of trauma. These are treatment activities aimed at moving children from feelings of responsibility to feelings of innocence.

It is necessary for an individual assessment of self-responsibility issues to be completed prior to the use of these activities.

There is ongoing clinical discussion concerning a child's need to feel responsible for abuse in order to defend against overwhelming feelings of vulnerability. This is a valid clinical concern and implies that clinicians be aware of this possibility when assessing issues of responsibility.

Treatment interventions that are designed to correct cognitive distortions may not have a significant impact. If a child persists in cognitive distortion, or if the clinical impression exists post-treatment that there has been no shift emotionally from the belief system, the issue of defense against vulnerability may be operating. Clearly, this defense must be preserved and the child referred for further work either individually or within the family system.

Particular circumstances may occur during post-assessment for which one would not attempt to correct a child's cognitive distortion regarding responsibility. Key clinical issues under these circumstances are safety and support. Is the child in a protected, safe setting, and are the child's supports operating for him or her? These two concerns would have to be addressed satisfactorily before any work on the vulnerability issue can be pursued.

Preschool – Latency
Kit's Story

MODALITY: Individual, group

GOAL: To educate young children about the concept of responsibility, and to transform feelings of guilt

MATERIALS

➤ Story: "Kit's Responsibility" *following*

➤ Picture of Kit *following*

➤ Crayons

➤ Coloring paper

METHOD

ADVANCE PREPARATION:
Make copies of Kit's picture for children to color and paper for them to draw pictures of Kit.

ACTIVITY:

The therapist reads Kit's story to the group. The therapist then engages the children in a dialogue by asking questions such as:

- How do you think Kit felt when Tom Cat told her to keep what happened a secret?
- Has something like this ever happened to you? Why did Kit feel responsible?
- Why do you think Tom Cat is responsible for what happened?

After the children discuss the story, they can draw a picture of their favorite part of the story, or color the picture of Kit.

DISCUSSION

Most children feel some degree of responsibility for the sexual abuse. They generally have an emotional belief about why they feel responsible. This belief may be due, in part, to the child's age and stage of development or to something said by the abuser. It is important to elicit what the children in the group see as Kit's understanding of why she was responsible.

This understanding will likely reflect their own perceptions. Kit's story can be used to teach children about the concept of responsibility and to alter the child's experience of self-blame. In processing the story, the therapist can reframe the children's feelings of self-blame by emphasizing how young and powerless children are.

The use of stories is helpful in treating young child victims, because stories are less threatening and they focus on influencing the child at an unconscious level. The aim of the activity is to develop a link between the character in the story and the child's own experience.

<u>STORY</u>

KIT'S RESPONSIBILITY

Once there was a little kitten who everybody called Kitty Cat, or Kit for short. Kit was very soft and furry. She had beautiful black fur with white patches on her cheeks and all the way up her two front paws. She had long, silky, white whiskers and her green eyes would sparkle when they caught the sunlight.

Kit loved to play with balls of yarn. She would push the balls along the ground with her nose or roll onto her back and bounce the yarn from side to side with her paws.

One day while Kit was rolling around with a big ball of red yarn, she got herself into a bit of a mess. The ball began to unravel and Kit became all tangled up in the yarn. The more she tried to untangle herself, the more knotted the yarn became.

Tom Cat, who was the big barn cat next door, saw what was happening and sauntered over to where Kit was ferveriously trying to untangle herself. "Do you need some help?" asked Tom. "Oh, yes," replied Kit, "I've gotten myself into a big tangle!"

So Tom Cat began to untangle Kit, but then something happened. Instead of pawing at the yarn, Tom started to paw at Kit. He pawed her fur all over, and began to purr in a strange way. Kit began to feel very uncomfortable. She knew this wasn't right—Mama Cat had taught her that nobody was to touch her like that. But she was too frightened to do anything. After a while, Tom said, "If you promise not to tell anyone about this, I will untangle you." "OK," replied Kit in a desperate tone. As Tom untangled Kit, he growled, "Remember, this will be our little secret!" And off he went, leaving Kit all alone and feeling very confused.

Kit didn't know what to do. She didn't like the way Tom had pawed at her, but she didn't think she should tell anyone because Tom Cat had made her promise to keep it a secret. Then Kit got a good idea. She decided to talk to her friend, the Wise Old Owl. He was very smart and could help her decide the right thing to do.

Kit found the Wise Old Owl in his usual spot, perched on the branch overlooking the meadow. "Well hoolow there my little Kit. What brings yhoo here twooday?"

"Oh, Mr. Owl, I have a big problem and I don't know what to do." Kit proceeded to tell the owl about what happened. "And it's all my fault because I didn't do anything to stop him."

"I can see how confusing this must seem, Kit, but yhoo must not blame yourself for something yhoo are not responsible for."

"What does responsible mean?"

"Responsible means something yhoo are in charge of. Just like the sun is responsible for giving us light and warmth, and the rain is responsible for filling our ponds and for giving us a little drink when we are thirsty. So Tom Cat is responsible for tricking yhoo by pretending to be nice and helpful at first and then touching yhoo where he is not supposed to. And he knows he has done something wrong because he told yhoo to keep it a secret so he will not get in trouble. You must tell your mama Cat and papa Cat about this because they are responsible for taking care of yhoo and for protecting yhoo. And do yhoo know what yhoo are responsible for?" "What?" asked Kit. "Yhoo are responsible for telling the truth, and yhoo are also responsible for remembering that yhoo are not to blame for this!"

Kit suddenly felt much better. Now she understood that what happened was not her responsibility. She was not to blame for what Tom Cat had done to her. So off she went to tell Mama and Papa Cat about what had happened. And as she trotted off, she thought to herself: Since it's my responsibility to tell the truth, I guess I better tell Mama and Papa about the time I chewed up Mr. Smith's favorite pair of socks!
The end.

PICTURE OF KIT

Latency
Guilt-Free Kids

MODALITY: Individual, group

GOAL: To challenge cognitive distortions related to feelings of guilt and to empower the child

M A T E R I A L S

➤ Comic book: "Gertie & Gordie: The Guilt-Free Kids" *following*

➤ Help Sheet *following*

➤ Colored pencils or markers

M E T H O D

ADVANCE PREPARATION:
Copy and staple the "Gertie and Gordie" pages together to form a comic book for each child.

ACTIVITY:
The therapist introduces the activity by stating: "When kids have been sexually abused, they often feel guilty, even if they have been told they are not to blame. Guilt feelings are stubborn and they may creep back again and again. Sometimes the guilt feelings occur because offenders trick kids into believing the abuse was their fault. Sometimes, when a child tells about the sexual abuse, people

246

respond in ways that make the child feel he/she has done something wrong. And, sometimes, kids feel guilty because of the way they think about what happened to them. See how good you are at helping Guilt-free Gertie and Guilt-free Gordie tell it like it is! For each of the cartoons in the comic book, write Gertie's or Gordie's response." An example can be shown to the children to illustrate. A Help Sheet is also provided to assist children in writing Gertie's and Gordie's responses.

DISCUSSION

Sexual victims internalize feelings of self-blame for various reasons. Children may feel guilty for the abuse itself, for having kept the abuse a secret, or for what happened at the time of disclosure. This activity presents various scenarios related to issues of responsibility, and creates a format for children to challenge and transform guilty feelings. The comic book format is a medium familiar to children, and provides emotional distance and humor to an otherwise difficult treatment theme.

HELP SHEET

- It's hard to say no when you're afraid.

- Every kid in the world loves attention.

- It's OK to cry when you're upset.

- Your family broke up because the abuser committed a crime.

- Nothing a person wears causes sexual abuse.

- Kids are afraid to tell they're being abused because they worry about what will happen if people find out about it.

- Abusers trick kids into going along with the sexual abuse by bribing them or offering them treats.

- It's hard for kids to say no because sexual abuse is confusing for kids.

- Kids go along with the sexual abuse because they are taught to obey adults.

- It's normal to feel good when parts of your body are touched.

- It's hard for kids to stop the abuse because they have less power than the abuser.

- Abusers trick kids into thinking the abuse was their idea.

- It's hard to say no to an adult you love.

- It's OK to still love the abuser.

- The abuser got in trouble because he did something wrong.

COMIC BOOK

Latency—Preteen
Who Is Responsible?

MODALITY: Individual, group

GOALS: To clarify thinking associated with feelings of guilt and responsibility; to reinforce the concept that child victims are not responsible for sexual abuse

MATERIALS

➤ Worksheet: "Who is Responsible" *following*

➤ Paper

➤ Pencils

➤ Chalkboard or flip chart

METHOD

ADVANCE PREPARATION:
Make copies of the worksheet and provide other materials for the group.

ACTIVITY:
The activity can be introduced by suggesting to the group that when bad things happen to you, sometimes it is hard to know when it's your fault. The group is divided into small groups and asked to complete a list of ten accidents or unfortunate mistakes. At this stage in the activity, the group should be told that the list cannot include anything about sexual abuse. If the group is having difficulty developing a list, the leader can offer an example such as: "You come out after school

and discover someone has stolen your bicycle."
The completed lists are shared with the whole group and together this
group decides where the responsibility lies. At this point in the
activity, the leader distributes copies of the "Who is Responsible"
worksheet.

In processing this activity, the following messages should be
introduced: *Sometimes kids make mistakes. Sometimes they forget a
rule or don't do everything the way they should. Sometimes they're
tricked into situations where they can be hurt or abused or taken
advantage of. Remember—no matter what happenes—KIDS ARE
NEVER NEVER TO BLAME FOR SEXUAL ABUSE—THAT'S THE
LAW.*

The last part of this activity consists of developing other lists, such as:
* 10 reasons why kids are never to blame for sexual abuse
* 10 tricks offenders use to confuse kids into thinking they
  are responsible
* 10 things I'd like to say to the person who abused me
* 10 things I'd like my supporters to say to me
* 10 reasons why kids should never be abused

DISCUSSION

The damaging aspects of feeling to blame for sexual abuse should be
addressed cognitively and emotionally. This activity helps to show
victims how understandable their feelings are. In addition to
normalizing feelings of guilt, it provides an opportunity to change
attitudes and beliefs about responsibility in general.

"Who is Responsible" begins by exploring situations that have no
connection to sexual abuse. Children are helped to understand that
feelings of sadness, helplessness, and powerlessness often lead to self-
blame and self criticism.

The most important part of this activity lies in processing group members' thoughts and feelings associated with the issue of responsibility.

CAUTION

Leaders should prepare group members for the probability that feelings of guilt may often return and cannot be reversed by attempts to understand and change attitudes. It is empowering for victims to know that their healing may be an uneven path and that whenever feelings of guilt and responsibility return, they have skills and resources to deal with them in positive ways.

WORSHEET

WHO IS RESPONSIBLE?

Read the situations below. For each situation, decide if it's your fault, somebody else's fault, or nobody's fault.

	Your fault	Someone else's fault	Nobody's fault
1. You are walking on the sidewalk and two bigger kids run by you and knock you down.	☐	☐	☐
2. You are in the school playground for recess. Someone trips you and you fall into the mud and get your clothes dirty.	☐	☐	☐
3. You leave your bicycle on the road and a car runs over it.	☐	☐	☐
4. A big girl tells you that she is going to give you some candy, but when you follow her to her back yard, she steals your new sweater.	☐	☐	☐
5. You forget to do your homework for school.	☐	☐	☐
6. You are sexually abused by a man who gives you money if you promise not to tell.	☐	☐	☐
7. You are running in your house and you knock a glass bowl onto the floor.	☐	☐	☐
8. You tell your mom you are going to the library, but you go to your friend's house. Some boys grab you and push you into the bedroom and touch your private parts.	☐	☐	☐
9. You forget to feed your dog.	☐	☐	☐
10. You are sexually abused by an uncle every time you go over to visit your grandparents. He says he is turned on by your tight jeans and your red sweater.	☐	☐	☐
11. There is a power failure and your alarm clock doesn't go off. This means you're late for school.	☐	☐	☐

Latency – Preteen
Guilt Trip

MODALITY: Group

GOALS: To assess the victim's perception of responsibility; to challenge cognitive distortions related to feelings of guilt; to reinforce the concept that children are not to blame for sexual abuse

MATERIALS

➤ Worksheet: "Guilt Quiz" *following*

➤ Game board: "Guilt Trip Game" *following*

➤ Guilt Erasers *following*

➤ Tagboard

➤ 1 small toy car

➤ Poster board

➤ Self-adhesive labels

➤ Markers, glitter

➤ Bumper Sticker Slogans *following*

➤ Pictures of cars *following*

METHOD

ADVANCE PREPARATION:
Copy the attached "Guilt Trip" game board onto a large piece of poster board or take it to a print shop and have it enlarged. Cut and paste the "Guilt Erasers" onto separate tagboard squares.

ACTIVITY:
The session begins by having each child complete the "Guilt Quiz." Next, the leader introduces the "Guilt Trip Game" by asking the group what a guilt trip is. If the children are having difficulty coming up with a response, then the leader can explain: "A guilt trip is when someone makes you feel guilty. For example, if the abuser says to the victim: 'You came to my house for a pizza party, so you must have wanted me to touch you,' then the abuser is trying to make the child feel responsible for the abuse—the abuser is giving the child a guilt trip."

The leader then explains that sexual abuse victims often feel guilty for aspects related to the abuse. This is a good opportunity to teach the children that guilt is a feeling that develops because of events that have happened to us and how we feel about those events. The concept of cognitive distortion can be illustrated using the following table:

EVENT	COGNITIVE DISTORTION	FEELING
Abuser says to victim: "You came to my house for a pizza party, so you must have wanted me to touch you."	*Child thinks:* The sexual abuse is my fault because I went to the abuser's house and I accepted treats form him.	Guilt

The leader then explains that the "Guilt Trip Game" is played to help children learn that they can change the way they think about the sexual abuse, so they don't feel they are to blame. The game is explained as follows: (*As this is a lengthy explanation, the leader may wish to copy it onto an instruction sheet for the kids to follow as the leader reads it aloud.*)

This game shows some things that may have happened to kids who have been sexually abused. One or more of these things may have happened to you. These things can make children feel guilty depending on how they think about them. As we move around the game board, we will have an opportunity to explore the reasons why kids often feel like the abuse is their fault. The game will help us to challenge these thoughts by using "guilt erasers." The "guilt erasers" help kids learn that they are not to blame for the sexual abuse.

The group members sit in a circle with the "Guilt Trip Game" board placed in the middle. The toy car is placed on the game board on the *Start* square. The leader distributes the "guilt erasers" to the group members. The "guilt erasers" should be evenly distributed among the group members.

The leader chooses one group member to begin the game. The first player moves the toy car along to the first square on the game board and reads the situation aloud to the group (i.e. "A kid kept the abuse a secret for a long time.") The leader asks the player, "What thoughts would a child have to make him feel guilty about having kept the abuse a secret?" Once the player has responded, the leader asks, "Who has a guilt eraser card that will challenge this child's feelings of guilt?" An example of an appropriate guilt eraser in this situation is: "Abusers trick kids into keeping the abuse a secret." The child reads the "guilt eraser" card aloud, and explains why he thinks it challenges the guilt. If the group members agree, then the player places the "guilt eraser" card on top of the square on the game board to cover the guilty statement.

The group member sitting to the left of the first player plays next, moving the toy car to the second square on the game board. The game continues until the car has completed the "guilt trip" and all the guilty situations on the game board have been covered, or "erased." The leader can encourage group cooperation by stating that it does not matter who gets rid of their "guilt eraser" cards first. It is only important that the group works together to complete the guilt trip.

As a closing activity, group members can make bumper stickers by selecting one of the Bumper Sticker Slogans and writing it on a decorated adhesive label. (Children can also make up their own slogans.) The bumper stickers can be stuck on a picture of a car. (Group members can use a copy of the car picture or cut one out from a magazine.)

DISCUSSION

This activity first teaches the concept of cognitive distortions, then helps children challenge and resolve their faulty thinking. The game is helpful in enabling children to begin to confront their feelings of self-blame. This game can be used as one of many strategies to address the children's feelings of responsibility for the sexual abuse. The issue of self-blame is complex and it is a long-term treatment issue for many victims of child sexual abuse. Children should not be left with the impression that once the guilt trip game is over, their feelings of self-blame will be permanently erased. Rather, children will recover more resiliently if they are taught that guilt feelings tend to persist and recur, and that they can employ strategies to deal with these uncomfortable feelings.

The impact of this activity is more powerful if the child's care giver is enlisted to play the "Guilt Trip Game" with the child to reinforce that the child is not to blame for the sexual abuse. The game can be played in a parallel, non-offending parent group session; or parents can be invited into the victim's group to play along with the child. This should only be done with care givers who have the capacity to provide genuine support to the child.

WORKSHEET

GUILT QUIZ

There are many reasons why kids blame themselves for the sexual abuse. Read each statement below and check off the ones that apply to you. Remember, there are no right or wrong answers—what's important is to show how <u>you</u> feel:

WHY I FEEL I AM TO BLAME

- ☐ I didn't say no.
- ☐ If I had told about the abuse sooner, I could have stopped it.
- ☐ I made it happen because I wore sexy clothes.
- ☐ I deserved what happened because I was bad.
- ☐ I kept going to see the abuser even though I knew the abuse would happen.
- ☐ I accepted money or presents from the abuser.
- ☐ I liked the special way the abuser treated me.
- ☐ Because I didn't tell sooner, the abuser abused someone else.
- ☐ I touched the abuser too.
- ☐ Parts of my body felt good when I was touched.
- ☐ I got the abuser in trouble.
- ☐ I broke up my family by telling.
- ☐ Since I told, everyone has been upset.
- ☐ I was taught not to let anyone touch my body, so I should have known to stop it.
- ☐ I had to go live in a foster home after I told.
- ☐ I told someone else about the abuse before I told my parents.
- ☐ Someone asked if I was being abused, and at first I lied and said no.
- ☐ Other reasons: _____

A kid thought she should say NO, but she didn't.

A kid was told not to go to the place where the abuse happened.

A kid was afraid to tell her family, so she told a friend first.

A kid was placed in a foster home.

A kid liked being treated special by the offender.

THE GUILT TRIP!

An offender gave a kid treats.

The family split up since the secret came out.

An offender said, "I'll stop if you really want me to."

The family feels the kid is making the whole thing up.

A kid took money from the offender.

The offender's family and friends believe the offender, not the kid.

A kid went back to see the offender after the abuse happened.

A kid was wearing sexy clothes and got abused.

Someone asked if a kid was being abused, but at first he/she lied and said no.

A kid felt pleasure during the sexual abuse.

Mom cried when she found out.

The offender asked the kid to touch him, and the kid obeyed.

A kid kept the secret for a long time.

The abuser got into trouble after the kid told.

START

People say the kid is a troublemaker.

FINISH

The offender went to jail.

A kid really loves the offender.

A kid knew other kids were being abused by the same offender.

GUILT ERASERS

It's hard for kids to break silence.	It hurts to see someone you love cry.	Kids keep the abuse secret because they worry what will happen if they tell.	Every kid in the world loves attention.
All kids want money.	Offenders trick kids.	All children love treats.	Kids go to foster homes so they'll be safe, not because they did something bad.
It's hard to say no to an adult you love.	Kids are taught to do what they're told.	Offenders are responsible for the abuse.	Kids worry about their parents' reaction if they tell.
Everyone likes to feel special.	The kid didn't split up the family, the offender did.	Offenders lie so they won't get in trouble.	Offenders say the kid is lying even though they're the ones who did something wrong.
Nobody deserves to be abused because of how he or she dresses or acts.	All bodies respond automatically to touch.	Abusers try different ways to convince kids to touch them.	Abusers trick kids into going along with sexual abuse.
Kids don't get abused because they are bad.	It's hard for kids to stop the abuse because they feel confused or scared.	It's OK to be angry and love the abuser at the same time.	All your feelings are OK.
Sexual abuse is a crime.	Sexual abuse is never a kid's fault.	Kids who tell about sexual abuse are brave.	Offenders sometimes threaten kids.

THE GUILT TRIP

This game generally engages otherwise resistant children and provides cognitive restructuring to neutralize feelings of guilt.

SLOGANS FOR BUMPER STICKERS

SEXUAL ABUSE IS NEVER A KID'S FAULT!
BOYS WHO TELL ABOUT SEXUAL ABUSE ARE HEROES!
GIRLS WHO TELL ABOUT SEXUAL ABUSE ARE SHEROES!
THERE IS NO LOVE IN SEXUAL ABUSE!
SEXUAL ABUSE IS AGAINST THE LAW!
ALL YOUR FEELINGS ARE OK!
ABUSERS KNOW SEXUAL ABUSE IS WRONG!
KIDS HAVE A RIGHT TO BE SAFE!
ALL CHILDREN ARE LOVABLE!

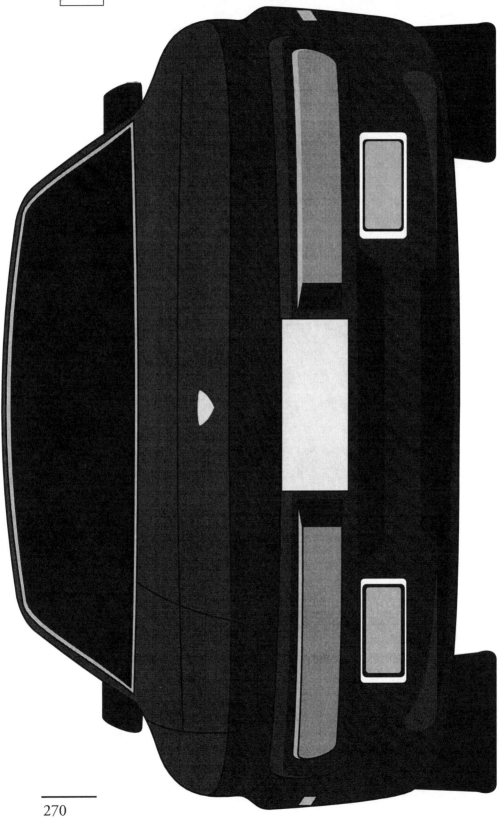

Latency – Teen

Why Me?

MODALITY: Individual, group

GOALS: To identify the victims' perspective on why they were chosen to be sexually abused, and to challenge cognitive distortions which contribute to feelings of responsibility for the sexual abuse

MATERIALS

➤ Worksheet: "Why Me?" *following*

➤ Poster board

➤ Strips of paper

➤ Scenarios: "Why Me?" *following*

➤ Index cards

➤ Envelopes

METHOD

ADVANCE PREPARATION:

The group leader makes a copy of the "Why Me?" worksheet for each group member and writes scenarios onto separate index cards. The following secret message is written onto a large piece of poster board: "Abusers molest kids because it feels good to them and they think they can get away with it." The 18 words in the secret message are covered with eighteen separate strips of paper.

ACTIVITY:

The therapist introduces the activity by telling the group that kids who have been sexually abused usually ask these questions:

- Why did this happen?
- Why me?

Group members can share if they have asked themselves such questions. Group members then complete the "Why Me?" worksheet. The completed worksheets are folded and placed in sealed envelopes.

Children take turns reading aloud the "Why Me" scenarios. As each scenario is discussed and the thinking of each victim is challenged and reframed, a different strip of paper is removed from the poster board. This continues until all eighteen strips of paper have been removed and the following secret message has been uncovered: "Abusers molest kids because it feels good to them and they think they can get away with it."

For the final part of the activity, group members are given back their sealed envelopes. Each group member opens an envelope, reads the response aloud to the group. Group members challenge and reframe the response. The therapist should ensure that the child who wrote the response has an opportunity to agree or disagree with the group and to ultimately decide the reason for being abused.

DISCUSSION

This is a complex treatment activity that requires great care in ensuring that sexual abuse victims receive appropriate messages about why they were sexually abused. The key points to clarify for children are:

- Offenders have the power to choose if and who they sexually abuse.
- A child does not choose to be sexually abused. (Children lack the developmental capacity to consent to sex.)
- Offenders typically deny their true intentions and try to rationalize their behavior to avoid feelings of responsibility.

The sequencing of the exercises in this session is important. The therapist must first assess the victim's belief system associated with why he or she thinks the abuse occurred, then shift the faulty thinking so that children understand that they are not responsible for being sexually abused.

WORKSHEET

WHY ME?

Do you ever wonder why the abuser decided to pick you? Write your thoughts in the word bubble below.

I think the offender sexually abused me because:

_____

_____

_____

_____

SCENARIOS: WHY ME?

- Ryan thought the abuser picked on him because the abuser wanted to hurt Ryan's mother.

- Latoya thought her stepfather molested her because she wasn't his "real" daughter.

- Sharon wondered if she was the only one of the five kids her dad sexually abused because she looked like her mother.

- Sylvia thought her teacher abused her because she was going to fail.

- Tommy wondered if his cousin sexually abused him because he looked gay.

- Dana thought she was molested because she wore sexy clothes.

- Jeff thought the offender picked him to sexually abuse because he was always in trouble and people thought he was "bad."

- Sheera wondered if she was sexually abused because she was pretty.

Latency – Teen
The Innocence of Childhood

MODALITY: Individual, group

GOALS: To help children understand they were not responsible for sexual abuse and to help children understand how they were manipulated to feel guilt and blame for the abuse

MATERIALS

➤ Pictures from family album (if available)

➤ Magazines

➤ Scissors

➤ Glue

➤ Attributes Statements *following*

METHOD

ADVANCE PREPARATION:
Collect magazines for use with this activity. Photocopy "Attributes Statements" for all group members.

ACTIVITY:
Leader asks children how many of them have pictures of themselves taken at the age when they were abused. If not all children have pictures, use magazines to cut out pictures of kids to represent themselves.

When group members have chosen their pictures, the group discusses the characteristics of children. Leader guides the group to identify such qualities as innocence, love of games, enjoyment of candy and toys, lack of knowledge and experience. Emphasis is placed on how trusting and dependent children are. Questions such as "When you were five, did you believe in the Tooth Fairy? What was your favorite toy? Were you allowed to cross the street by yourself?" The children can then rewrite a story about their pictures, titled *When I Was Little*. This will capture their innocence at the time.

Ask the group to think about how easy it is for an adult to take advantage of a child.

The last part of the activity is for group members to choose Attributes Statements that apply to them. They are to cut and glue statements to the picture of themselves.

DISCUSSION

Through this activity, children can get in touch with their victim status. The self-destructive feelings are challenged. The reality of how vulnerable and trusting they were and how the offender misused their trust and exploited their vulnerability is clarified in a most powerful way.

Providing visual, concrete ways for children to view themselves can be useful in externalizing confusing or distorted self-imagery.

ATTRIBUTES STATEMENTS

I was an innocent child.
I was not able to say "no."
The abuser knew it was wrong.
The abuser was bigger.
The abuser was stronger.
The abuser was powerful.
I was forced.
I was tricked.
My feelings were confused.
I was afraid.
I thought I could trust the abuser.
I was confused by my body's reactions.
I was afraid to tell anybody.

The abuser gave me special attention.
The abuser bribed me with treats or presents.
I loved the abuser.
The abuser was fun to be with.
I thought adults had to be obeyed.
I felt I just couldn't say no.
I was little.
The abuser acted like nothing happened.

MY FEELINGS WERE CO—

I WAS AN INNOCENT CHILD

I FELT I JUST COULDN'T SAY NO

I WAS TRICKED

THE ABUSER WAS BIGGER

I THOUGHT I COULD TRUST THE ABUSER

I was four when Grandpa started to sexually abuse me. I only told my teddy bear about the secret. It all started when Grandpa gave me the red cowboy hat for my birthday. He said I was his "special cowgirl!" He made up games that started out fun, but then turned yucky. I was really confused back then, but now I know he tricked me just so he could get his kicks!

THE INNOCENCE OF CHILDHOOD

Children make contact with their innocence and vulnerability by doing this exercise. It is a powerful way to clarify the victim-offender status.

PAPER DOLLS AND PAPER AIRPLANES

Preteen – Teen
Talk Back

MODALITY: Individual, group

GOAL: To challenge cognitive distortions related to feelings of guilt, and to empower the child

MATERIALS

➤ Cartoon Bubble Sheets *following*

➤ Handout: "How The Abuser Tried to Make Me Feel Responsible" *following*

➤ Handout: "Talk Back Statements" *following*

➤ Construction paper

➤ Glue sticks

➤ Scissors

➤ Stapler

METHOD

ADVANCE PREPARATION:
Make copies of the Cartoon Bubble Sheets and both Handouts.

282

ACTIVITY:

This activity can be introduced with a statement that most kids who have been sexually abused feel guilty — they feel like it's their fault. The therapist explains that many of the reasons why sexual victims feel guilty has to do with something the abuser may have said or did. The leader can offer an example to illustrate this point: "If the abuser tells you that he is touching you because of the sexy bathing suit you are wearing, then he is trying to place the blame on you, so the abuser can convince himself that he is not responsible for the sexual abuse."

The therapist then holds up a sample cartoon with an example of what an abuser may say to a victim .

The group takes the offender's statement and deconstructs it with questions like: "Why would an offender say to a child 'If you didn't want me to touch you, you wouldn't have accepted the chocolate bar!" "How would this statement affect a victim?" "What information would neutralize these guilt feelings?" "What could the victim say to the abuser to shift the responsibility onto the abuser?" A chart can be developed to illustrate:

WHAT ABUSERS SAY	HOW IT AFFECTS THE VICTIM	THE TRUTH
"If you didn't want me to touch you, you wouldn't have accepted the chocolate bar."	Makes the child feel like it was his/her fault.	The abuser tricked the child into going along with the abuse by bribing the child.

The therapist then distributes a set of cartoon bubble sheets to each group member. Group members read each cartoon and select which offender statements apply to their situation. Children should also be provided with blank bubble cartoons to add what the abuser said to them.

Children then respond to the abuser or "talk back" to the abuser by writing a response in the blank cartoon bubble. Children can make up their own responses, or use any of the statements from the handout: "What Do You Say to a Sex Offender." The purpose of this part of the activity is to help victims respond to the messages of blame they have received from the abuser and to shift the responsibility where it belongs—onto the abuser.

If desired, children can color in the cartoons. The cartoons are then stapled together to form a comic book. The child then creates a cover for the comic book by selecting a title and then decorating the page.

DISCUSSION

Children often feel overwhelmed at the thought of protesting or challenging a person who victimized them. This activity encourages victims to "talk back" to the abuser to enable them to find a voice and to challenge the power of the abuser's manipulative messages. The activity will help children to recognize how abusers attempt to trick victims into accepting responsibility for the abuse, and it will help children to place the responsibility back onto the abuser.

HANDOUT

HOW THE ABUSER TRIED TO MAKE ME FEEL RESPONSIBLE

I thought you wanted me to do it.
I can tell you like this because your body responds when I touch you.
If you really wanted me to stop, you would have said something when I started rubbing your back.
If you didn't want me to touch you, why did you take the money?
You kept coming back for more.
If you didn't want me to do this, you wouldn't wear those sexy clothes.
I can tell by the way you're breathing you really like me to do this to you.
I thought you were asleep and wouldn't notice.
I thought you'd tell me to stop.
Why did you skip school and come over here if you didn't want to have sex?

You've had sex with other people. What's the big deal? You're not a virgin.

You're in so much trouble, this will make you feel better. Even if you told, no one would believe you.

If you really loved your mother, you wouldn't be having sex with me.

What we're doing would really break your mother's heart. For her sake we have to keep it a secret.

People just don't understand how much we love each other. We'll have to keep it a secret till you're all grown-up!

HANDOUT

TALK BACK STATEMENTS

You used my loyalty to my family to trick me!
You used your strength to force me.
You used my love for my mother to keep me quiet.
You used my fear of being put in a foster home to make me keep the secret.
You made it impossible for me and my mother to feel close.
You stole my childhood.
You committed a crime.
You bribed me to make me feel guilty.
You gave me special attention which confused me.
You betrayed my trust.
You knew what you were doing was wrong.
You knew I was afraid no one would believe me.
You knew I was afraid that I would get in trouble.

You knew I loved you and didn't want anything bad to happen to you.
You knew that I was afraid our family would break up.
You knew I was embarrassed about being abused.
You didn't care how I felt. You just cared about what you were doing.
You thought I would never tell.
I didn't know how to say "No!"
Bodies respond automatically to touch.
I was afraid to say anything because I was powerless in the situation.
My cooperation was bribed.
There were reasons why I couldn't get the abuse to stop – I didn't know how to get out of the situation.
What I wear has nothing to do with why you abused me.
I was so frightened I could hardly catch my breath.
I pretended to be asleep so you would go away.

I was afraid, and I didn't know how to stop the abuse.

No matter where I am or who I'm with, I have the right to say "no" to touch I don't want.

I have the right to choose who I want to share my body with.

I was so afraid that no one would believe me, I couldn't say "no."

You drove a wedge between my mother and me and made it hard for me to communicate with her.

You forced my cooperation and made me feel guilty.

You tried to make me feel it was my idea.

CARTOON BUBBLE SHEET

CARTOON BUBBLE SHEET

CARTOON BUBBLE SHEET

Chapter 9
Offenders

PURPOSE OF THIS CHAPTER:

The clinical focus of this chapter is on the betrayal of trust. This key dynamic of sexual abuse has the potential to affect the child's future relationships. For this reason, the following activities have been developed to examine in detail the relationship between child and offender within the context of betrayal.

Establishing a cognitive framework that allows the child to understand the concepts of trickery, coercion, and manipulation, provides the groundwork for the emotional shifts necessary in assigning responsibility to the offender. Inherent in this work is the knowledge of the inequality of the abuser/victim relationship and power differentials that allow for the imposition of secrecy, keeping the child isolated from help and support.

It is important for therapists to be attuned to the sensitive issue of the child's vulnerability and the child's perceived feelings of helplessness. Therapists need to be aware that some of the child's feelings of responsibility may be a defense against these feelings. It is therefore imperative that therapists track the ease or difficulty with which children process this series of activities.

Therapists also need to be aware that children often assign reasons like "the abuser was sick," "the abuser was drunk," or "the abuser made a mistake" to explain the behavior of the offender. This conclusion may be their own, or it may have been stated by the family or by the offender. The clinical concern regarding this reasoning is that it does not allow the child to assign full responsibility for the abuse to the offender. By using the reasons stated above, the why of the abuse becomes illness, alcohol, or a mistake rather than the abuser's responsiblity. From a therapeutic standpoint, the felt innocence of the child is important to the child's recovery. This innocence can be undermined unless responsibility is completely assigned to the offender.

Answering the question "Why?" is complex. The activities in this chapter are designed to answer broadly why offenders offend. What is clinically important is to keep the focus on the offender's decision to offend and make certain the child does not feel that he/she did anything to contribute to the abuse. Again, whatever perceptions the child has regarding "cooperation" should be identified in the Trauma Assessment.

Preschool
Little Red Riding Hood

MODALITY: Individual, group

GOALS: To gain skills in identifying tricks, manipulation, and coercion that offenders use to get children to cooperate with the secret touching; to empower victims; to give children sense of control

MATERIALS

➤ Simple Magic Trick

➤ Story of "Little Red Riding Hood"

➤ Drawing paper

➤ Markers, crayons

METHOD

ADVANCE PREPARATION:
Practice a simple magic trick until you can do it well in front of the children.

ACTIVITY:
Begin by conducting a magic trick, followed by a discussion of why people play tricks: "Why do we like tricks? Why do they work? Have you ever played a trick on somebody?" Then introduce the story of "Little Red Riding Hood" by saying it is the story of a very clever trickster.

Read the story to the group, stopping to ask questions and get ideas from the children. *What trick confused Red Riding Hood? What trick frightened her?* Then relate the concept of tricks to sexual abuse. Lead a discussion about how sometimes tricks make kids feel guilty, confused, and/or frightened. Explain the difference between the fun tricks in a magic show, and the scary or confusing tricks in secret touching.

Following the discussion, children can draw pictures of how they were tricked into secret touching.

DISCUSSION

Very young children understand the concept of tricks. They enjoy magic, mystery, and magicians. The idea of feeling confused or hurt by a trick is an important concept to introduce at this age because it forms the cornerstone of personal safety.

Preschoolers can brainstorm ideas of what they might do if someone played a mean trick on them. Care givers can be enlisted for role-playing situations.

Preschool—Latency
The Abuser's Bag of Tricks

MODALITY: Individual, group

GOAL: To help children understand and identify the enticement strategies used by their offenders

MATERIALS

➤ 2 puppets

➤ 1 paper lunch bag per child

➤ Strips of paper

➤ Handout: "Common Tricks Used by Sexual Abusers" (if needed)

➤ Instructions for "The Magic Balloon" *following*, balloon, masking tape, and pin

METHOD

ADVANCE PREPARATION:
Copy the handout for distribution. Gather puppets to use in this activity.

ACTIVITY:
Group leaders perform a puppet show for the children, using two puppets—one puppet represents the abuser and the other puppet represents the victim. We generally use a wolf puppet and a rabbit

puppet. (If used in individual therapy, the therapist should play both roles.) The aim of the puppet show is to illustrate the concept of enticement strategies (see attached script and discussion questions). The discussion following the puppet show should be focused on how kids are sometimes tricked into doing things they don't want to do. The therapist can ask the group for ways that kids are tricked by people who touch them. The therapist can stress the concept that abusers know kids are scared and uncomfortable.

This discussion leads into a craft activity called "The Abuser's Bag of Tricks." Each child is provided with a paper bag and several strips of blank paper. Children begin by writing "The Abuser's Bag of Tricks" on the front of their paper bag.

Children write on their slips of paper different things their abuser said or did to get them to go along with the sexual abuse and to keep it a secret. The slips of paper are then placed in the paper bag. The handout "Common Tricks Used by Sexual Abusers" can be provided to help children who are having difficulty identifying enticement strategies. Children can use this handout by cutting out the statements that apply to their situation.

The therapist can modify this activity for preschoolers by having them draw pictures of how the abuser tricked them and placing the pictures in the paper bag. Each child's care giver can read the list of "common tricks" to the child and, if any apply, the child can cut them out and place them in the bag along with the picture.

As a closing activity, the leader can teach the children "The Magic Balloon" magic trick (see following). It is important that the leader differentiate between tricks that are fun and safe and tricks that are scary and unsafe. For more ideas on teaching magic tricks to children, refer to *Give A Magic Show* (Burton and Rita Marks, New York: William Morrow & Co., Inc.,1977).

DISCUSSION

An important aspect of the sexual abuse victim's healing process is to understand that perpetrators plan the abuse and employ various enticement strategies to gain the child's cooperation. In processing this activity, the therapist should stress just how tricky abusers can be to reinforce the concept of offender responsibility. Once children can understand that they were deceived and manipulated by the abuser, they can perceive the abuser as responsible.

Discussion Questions for Enticement Strategy Role-Play

The leader should ask the group members the following questions after the role play:

- What did the wolf say or do to get the bunny to go along with him?

- How was the bunny feeling?

- Why was it hard for the bunny to just say no?

- Why would it be hard for the bunny to tell someone about this?

- Do abusers use tricks to get kids to go along with the secret touching? What kinds of tricks do abusers use?

This activity was developed for the Crisis Support Group Program at the Metropolitan Toronto Special Committee on Child Abuse and is being used with permission.

SCRIPT:
ENTICEMENT STRATEGY ROLE PLAY

Wolf: "Hello there, Bunny. How are you today?"

Bunny: "Fine, how are you?"

Wolf: "Well, I'm kind of bored. How would you like to come with me to play by the train tracks?"

Bunny: "I'm not allowed to go there because it's dangerous."

Wolf: "I won't tell anyone if you come with me."

Bunny: "Well, I don't think it's a good idea."

Wolf: "Oh, come on, it will be our little secret and we'll just go this one time."

Bunny: "I'm really not supposed to."

Wolf: "But you're my special friend. I can go with somebody else, but I'd rather play with you. And besides, if you won't go, I won't be your friend anymore and I'll tell everyone that you're a loser!"

Bunny: "Well I don't want you to do that."

Wolf: "So then come on. I'll even get you a special treat if you come with me. Come on, I know you want to."

Bunny: "Gee, I don't know what to do."

Wolf: "No one has to find out. It will be our special secret. You can trust me!"

Bunny: "Well ...OK."

HANDOUT

COMMON TRICKS USED BY SEXUAL ABUSERS

Tricks are what abusers say or do to get kids to go along with the sexual abuse or to keep it a secret. Abusers are very tricky. They know what to do or say to get kids to cooperate with them. Below is a list of tricks that abusers often use.

They make sure nobody else is around.

They make it a secret.

They bribe the child with treats or presents.

They scare or threaten the child.

They make the child feel sorry for the abuser.

They call it a game and make it appear fun.

They make it look like it's the child's fault.

They make the child feel special.

They act nice.

They convince the child it was an accident.

They win the child's trust.

They wait until the child is asleep.

They convince the child it was just a dream.

They tell the child it's sex education.

They make the child feel guilty.

They convince the child it's OK.

BAG OF TRICKS

Group leaders have as much fun as the kids hamming it up in the Enticement Strategy puppet show.

THE MAGIC BALLOON

ADVANCE PREPARATION:

Blow up a balloon, then put two pieces of masking tape on the balloon to make an X. When your audience is ready, show them the balloon but hide the taped portion of the balloon from them. Make a big production to introduce your trick by bragging about your skills and talents as a magician. Stick the pin through the X. The balloon won't pop because the tape holds it together!

Most of the fun and success of magic tricks depend upon how the magician or trickster presents them. Costume and props are important. You might want to work on your routine and practice your "abracadabra" magic spells!

Preschool – Latency
Hot Potato

MODALITY: Group

GOAL: To enable children to talk about their perception of the abuser

MATERIALS

➤ Index cards

➤ A potato

METHOD

ADVANCE PREPARATION:
The therapist copies the following questions onto index cards (one question per index card):

- What is your favorite toy?

- What is your favorite flavor of ice cream?

- If you had one wish, what would you wish for?

- What is something that makes you feel happy?

- What is something that makes you feel sad?

- Who is the person who touched your private parts?

- What is something the abuser said to you?

- What is something you want to say to the abuser?

- What do you think your mom/parents would want to say to the abuser?

ACTIVITY:

The children sit crossed-legged in a circle, facing the group leader who is seated in the middle. The index cards are placed in a stack (in the order listed above) in the middle of the circle. The leader starts the game by throwing the potato to a player, and then closes her eyes once the game is under way. (The leader must close her eyes so she can't tell who has the potato at any given time.)

The first player catches the hot potato and tosses it to the person to the immediate left. The game continues with the hot potato getting tossed around the circle. If the potato is tossed out of play, the last person to touch it must retrieve it.

After a short period, the leader shouts, "Hot potato!" The player caught holding the potato at that moment must answer the question that the leader picks from the stack of cards. Once one child has answered the question, the person to that child's immediate left must answer the same question, and so on until all the group members have had a turn to respond to the question. The potato is again passed around the group until the leader shouts, "Hot potato." The person who is caught with the potato answers the second question and then the other group members answer the question. The game continues until all the questions have been answered.

A fun closing activity is to have the children make "potato people." Children can use raw unpeeled potatoes, toothpicks, pipe cleaners, construction paper, raisins and other edible items to create their own characters!

DISCUSSION

Many children will already be familiar with the game of "Hot Potato." It is a simple game that will stimulate enthusiasm in the group and will help the children verbalize their feelings about the abuser. It is important that the game begin with questions that are less threatening to ease the children into self-disclosure.

Latency
Pit Stop

MODALITY: Individual, group

GOAL: To introduce the concept of offender tricks and
manipulation and help children understand the
relationship between enticement strategies and feelings
of self-blame

MATERIALS

➤ Worksheet: "Pit Stop" *following*

➤ Magic trick book

➤ Toy cars

METHOD

ADVANCE PREPARATION:
Practice a magic trick so you will be ready to do it in front of the
group. Make copies of the worksheet to use in this activity.

ACTIVITY:
The leader selects a magic trick from the magic trick book and
performs it for the children. This leads into a discussion about tricks
and the difference between fun, safe tricks and tricks that are used to
manipulate for sexual purposes. Children then complete the "Pit
Stop" Worksheet and share their responses with the group.

As a fun closing activity, the group members can design a racetrack game using a homemade racetrack and toy cars.

DISCUSSION

This activity is most appealing to young boys. It has been consistently reported by leaders of boys' groups that management and behavior control is more of an issue than with girls' groups. By making an activity appealing and less threatening and by considering the interests of boys, behavior management issues are lessened and the attention span of children is increased.

PAPER DOLLS AND PAPER AIRPLANES

WORKSHEET

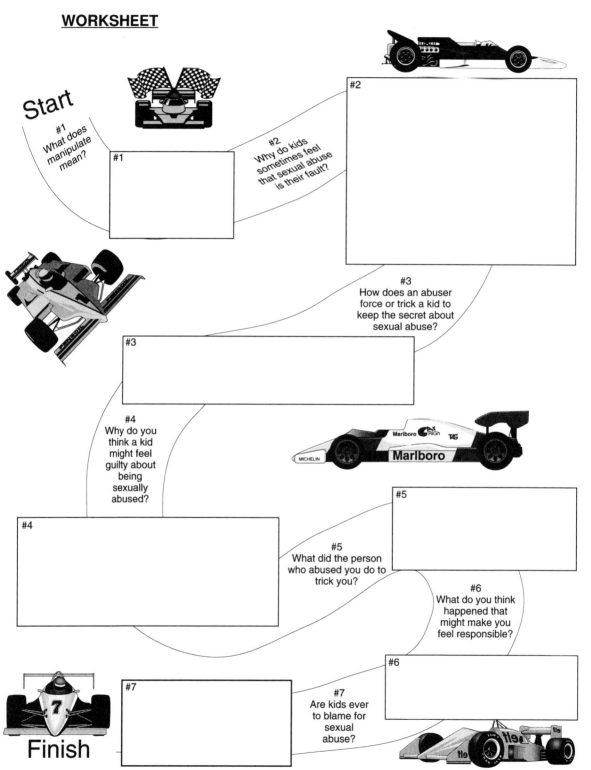

Start

#1
What does manipulate mean?

#1

#2
Why do kids sometimes feel that sexual abuse is their fault?

#2

#3
How does an abuser force or trick a kid to keep the secret about sexual abuse?

#3

#4
Why do you think a kid might feel guilty about being sexually abused?

#4

#5
What did the person who abused you do to trick you?

#5

#6
What do you think happened that might make you feel responsible?

#6

#7
Are kids ever to blame for sexual abuse?

#7

Finish

310

Latency—Teen
Types & Tricks of Abusers

MODALITY: Individual, group

GOAL: To enable children to identify the manipulative characteristics of their abusers and to help children view abusers as responsible

MATERIALS

➤ Worksheet: "Types & Tricks of Abusers" *following*

➤ List: "Things Abusers May Say to Kids" *following*

➤ 6 envelopes

➤ Paper bag

METHOD

ADVANCE PREPARATION:
The therapist labels the front of each envelope with a different abuser type: *Nice Abuser, Mean Abuser, Sneaky Abuser, Sad Abuser, Blaming Abuser, Lying Abuser.* The "Things Abusers May Say to Kids" list is cut into strips, so that each statement is on a separate slip of paper. These are placed in a bag.

ACTIVITY:

The activity is introduced with the following skit:

The therapist gives one of the group members a pencil. The therapist states that she is going to try different ways to try to get the child to give her the pencil. The children must guess which approach the therapist is using (nice, mean, sneaky, sad, blaming, or lying). The therapist can follow the script below:

<u>Nice</u>:	"You're my special friend. I'm sure you wouldn't mind giving me your pencil and if you give it to me, I'll buy you a chocolate bar!"
<u>Mean</u>:	"If you don't give me the pencil, I'll beat you up!"
<u>Sad</u>:	"I'm too poor to buy a pencil. Do you think you could give me yours?"
<u>Sneaky/lying/blaming</u>:	"You stole that pencil from me. Give it back!"

The therapist asks group members to identify the approaches and tricks used to get the child to hand over the pencil. The therapist states: "When somebody wants to convince you to do something, he or she may try different ways to get you to go along with it. They may act nice or mean; they may try to bribe, trick, or force you. People who sexually abuse kids use different ways to trick kids into going along with the abuse and to keep it a secret."

For the second part of the activity, group members take turns selecting from the bag a slip of paper with a statement from the "Things Abuser's Say to Kids" list. The group members must determine what type of abuser would make that statement and then place that statement in the appropriate envelope. For example, "Do as I say or I will hurt you" would go into the envelope marked *Mean*

Abuser while "You're my special friend" would go into the envelope marked *Nice Abuser* or in the envelope marked *Sneaky Abuser*.
The final part of the activity consists of the children completing the "Types & Tricks of Abusers" Worksheet.

DISCUSSION

In order to help sexual victims view the abuser as perpetrator, victims need to understand that abusers employ different strategies to entice, manipulate, control, and trick them. This is particularly important for children who developed a special relationship with the abuser and who have conflicting feelings toward the abuser. This activity helps children to understand that all abusers use tricks and manipulation, regardless of whether they have a friendly or coercive approach.

If this activity is being used with children who will be testifying against the abuser in criminal court proceedings, then it is suggested that the second part of the activity be eliminated, as defense attorneys may claim that the therapist unduly influenced the child.

This activity was developed for the Crisis Support Group Program at the Metropolitan Toronto Special Committee on Child Abuse and is being used with permission.

WORKSHEET
A B U S E R S : T Y P E S & T R I C K S

Circle the abuser most like the one who abused you. (you can circle more than one since some abusers act in different ways). Fill in the word bubbles by writing the things that the abuser said to you:

NICE ABUSER:
Tricked me by being friendly, treating me special, giving me treats

MEAN ABUSER:
Tricked me by scaring me, threatening me, forcing me

SNEAKY ABUSER:
Tricked me by abusing me when nobody else was around

SAD ABUSER:
Tricked me by making me feel sorry for him

BLAMING ABUSER:
Tricked me by convincing me it was my fault

LYING ABUSER:
Tricked me by lying to me

LIST

THINGS ABUSERS MAY SAY TO KIDS

- "You're my special friend."
- "Do as I say or I will hurt you."
- "We'll wait until nobody is around, then we'll play the touching game."
- "I feel so lonely, I need you to touch me."
- "You made me do this because of the sexy dress you wore."
- "Your parents said this way OK."
- "Don't tell anyone about this. It will be our special secret."
- "If you do as I say, I'll buy you that bike you really want."
- "If you tell I will go to jail, your mother will get sick, and you will be taken away."
- "I'll teach you about sex so you'll know what to do when you have a boyfriend."
- "You're so pretty, I can't stop myself from touching you."
- "It's OK, you can trust me."
- "Nothing happened, you were just dreaming."
- "I'm doing this because I love you."
- "I picked you out of all the kids because I like you the best."
- "Why stop if it feels good?"
- "Your parents will be angry at you if you tell them how you touched me like this."
- "I wouldn't do this if I didn't think you really wanted me to."
- "If you don't do this, I will touch your sister instead."
- "This is what two people do to show they love each other."

Latency—Teen
Scavenger Hunt

MODALITY: Group

GOAL: To assess the relationship between the victim and the abuser from the child's point of view, and to provide the child with an opportunity to express feelings about the abuser in a non-threatening way

MATERIALS

➤ Booklet: "Scavenger Hunt" *following*

➤ Magazine pictures

➤ Glue sticks

➤ Scissors

METHOD

ADVANCE PREPARATION:
Make copies of the booklet to use in this activity. You may also provide a variety of magazines that have a lot of pictures.

ACTIVITY:
The therapist begins by ascertaining that all children understand the concept of a scavenger hunt. For example, the leader can ask group members, "Who has ever been on a scavenger hunt?" and group members can share their experiences. If the group is unfamiliar with scavenger hunts, the leader must explain the rules. The leader then distributes the scavenger hunt booklets (one per group member), and

the children complete them by searching for the appropriate pictures from magazines (or group members can draw their own pictures to represent their feelings).

A fun way to close this activity is to divide the group into two teams and to have the teams compete to find the following scavenger hunt items. The leader can use this sample list of scavenger hunt items or create one to fit the needs and age level of the group members.

SCAVENGER HUNT ITEMS

- Pair of white socks
- Someone who has a birthday in the spring
- An outline of a hand
- A watch
- A drawing of the group leader
- A giant bubble gum bubble
- A verse from a nursery rhyme
- A smiling face

DISCUSSION

Offenders and their victims' feelings about them combine to make a highly charged emotional issue. This activity lowers the threat level and facilitates expression of feelings.

When the activity is shared among group members, the leader has an opportunity to stress that all people have different feelings and that all feelings are OK.

Victims will express a variety of feelings toward abusers, including feelings of hatred, love, or ambivalence. The leader is cautioned to be very accepting of any feelings the group members express, and to be ready to deal with reactive statements from group members, such as "How can you love someone who sexually abused you?"

BOOKLET

SCAVENGER HUNT

Find a picture that reminds
you of the abuser.

Find a picture that shows how
you feel about the abuser.

Find a picture that shows how
your support person thinks
about the abuser.

Find a picture that shows how
the abuser feels about you

Preteen—Teen
Abusers Know Kids

MODALITY: Individual, group

GOAL: To enable sexual victims to identify the manipulative strategies used by the abuser to entice them into the abuse and keep it a secret, and to help victims view the abuser as responsible

MATERIALS

➤ Scenarios: "Abusers Know Kids" *following*

➤ Chart: "Abusers Know Kids" *following*

METHOD

ADVANCE PREPARATION:
Make copies of the scenarios to use with the children.

ACTIVITY:
The group is divided into pairs. Each pair is provided with a scenario. The pairs are to identify what the abuser knew about the child in the scenario and how the abuser used that knowledge to manipulate the child into the abuse. The pairs share their scenario and their responses with the rest of the group. (If this activity is being used in individual therapy, then the therapist and client work together on one scenario.)

The therapist provides each child with the "Abusers know kids" chart. Children are to check off on the chart what they think their abuser knew about them and which strategies their abuser used to entice them into the sexual abuse.

DISCUSSION

This activity takes a psychoeducational approach by helping victims understand the nature and etiology of offender enticement strategies. It is important for victims to understand that sexual abusers exploit the innocence and powerlessness of children to trick them into the sexual abuse. Victims who are able to comprehend that they were innocent and vulnerable will be able to view the abuser as responsible for having manipulated them into the sexual abuse.

SCENARIOS

A B U S E R S   K N O W   K I D S

Brian is a shy child with few friends. His parents are divorced and Brian hardly ever gets to see his father, because his father moved away after the breakup of the marriage. Brian loves to play baseball, even though he is not very good at sports. For his birthday, Brian's mother bought him a baseball glove and enrolled Brian in a baseball league. Brian's coach, Steve, took a special interest in Brian and allowed Brian to stay after baseball practice for extra batting lessons. Steve also gave Brian a baseball hat. One day after baseball practice, when the other kids had left, Steve took Brian into the sports shed and sexually abused him. Afterwards, Steve told Brian that if he promised not to tell, he would let Brian play first base.

What did Steve know about Brian, and how did he use this knowledge to get Brian to go along with the sexual abuse and to keep it a secret?

Every Thursday evening when Marcy's mother would go out to play bingo, Marcy's stepfather, Tom, would sexually abuse her. Tom told Marcy that if she didn't go along with the sexual abuse, he would begin to abuse her little sister. Tom also told Marcy that if she told, he would lose his job and go to jail, and the family would be poor.

What did Tom know about Marcy, and how did he use this knowledge to get Marcy to go along with the sexual abuse and to keep it a secret?

325

One night during a terrible thunderstorm, Katie became frightened and went into her parents' bed. She woke up later to find her father touching her vagina. She asked him what he was doing. He told her she was just having a bad dream and to go back to sleep.

What did Katie's father know about Katie, and how did he use this knowledge to trick Katie into the sexual abuse and to keep it a secret?

One day, Susan was playing with her ball inside the house, even though her mother told her not to. The ball bounced onto the table and broke the vase. Her older brother threatened to tell their parents unless she agreed to touch his penis.

What did Susan's brother know about her, and how did he use this knowledge to trick her into the sexual abuse and to keep it a secret?

CHART

A B U S E R S   K N O W   K I D S

Sexual abusers know a lot about kids. They use what they know about kids to trick them. How did your abuser use his/her knowledge of kids to trick and manipulate you?

WHAT ABUSERS KNOW ABOUT KIDS	HOW ABUSERS USE THIS KNOWLEDGE TO TRICK KIDS
Kids love getting treats and presents.	Abusers bribe kids by giving them treats or presents.
Kids are loyal to good friends.	Abusers develop special friendships with victims.
All kids need attention.	Abusers give kids special attention.
Kids like to be told they're pretty.	Abusers compliment kids.
Kids get scared if they are threatened.	Abusers threaten kids.
Kids like to be around people who are nice to them.	Abusers act nice to kids.
Kids like to play games.	Abusers know lots of fun games.
Kids will do anything for people they feel sorry for.	Abusers tell kids they feel lonely, sick, or upset.
Kids can be easily convinced, especially by an adult.	Abusers convince kids that what they are doing is OK.

WHAT ABUSERS KNOW ABOUT KIDS	HOW ABUSERS USE THIS KNOWLEDGE TO TRICK KIDS
Kids feel guilty if they are told they are bad.	Abusers convince kids it's their fault.
Kids are taught to obey adults.	Abusers say, "Don't tell."
Kids are afraid to lose their families.	Abusers tell kids they will go to a foster home if people find out.
Kids are embarrassed to talk about sex.	Abusers just do it because they know kids will find it hard to talk about it.
Kids don't like to make their mothers cry.	Abusers tell kids their mothers will be upset if the secret comes out.
Kids don't like to get in trouble.	Abusers tell kids they will be punished if people find out.
Kids trust adults.	Abusers do it when nobody else is around because kids will listen to them.

Chapter 10
Triggers

PURPOSE OF THE CHAPTER:
Triggers are stimuli which result in a sensory-based reliving of some aspect of the sexual abuse experience. Triggers are often unconscious, but they can develop into phobic reactions which dominate a child's functioning and can take on a life of their own.

These sensitivities are often most clearly identified in preteen and adolescent children. It is important, therefore, to introduce the concept earlier in the child's development. Introducing language and information regarding how the body responds becomes therapeutically useful prior to preteen development. Normalizing sensory reactions and providing tools for children to deal with these reactions is part of this therapeutic intervention.

Concepts introduced by Hindman (1989), such as "bleeding-out" potent triggers and "neutralizing" the effects are incorporated into the theoretical underpinnings of the activities in this chapter.

For some children, triggers will be a focalizing point for the effects of the abuse experience. In this case, these children may need further, more intensive work in this area.

Preschool – Latency
Yucky & Nice

MODALITY: Individual, group

GOAL: To introduce a way for young children to put words to their negative associations to the abuse experience and to help children counter phobic reactions to these triggers

MATERIALS

➤ Magazines with a variety of pictures

➤ Scented stickers

➤ Cardboard or pre-made badge holders (available from office supply stores)

➤ Scissors

➤ Glue

➤ Markers

➤ Props (see Methods Section below for explanation)

METHOD

ADVANCE PREPARATION:
The therapist prepares a variety of props that will help to explain the concept of triggers to young children. The therapist cuts out pictures

from magazines that represent "yucky" things and "nice" things. For example, a spider for "yucky" and a kitten for "nice" or a garbage dump for "yucky" and a flower garden for "nice."

ACTIVITY:

The therapist introduces the activity by showing the children the "yucky" and "nice" props. Different feelings and reactions are elicited from the children. For example, "Do we feel yucky or nice when we see the spider? Is the picture of the kitten yucky or nice?" Children can be encouraged to give their own examples of yucky and nice.

The therapist then asks: "When you think of the secret touching, was it yucky or nice? What was yucky about it?" The children are then provided with magazines to find pictures of things that are "yucky" or representations of their negative triggers. Children glue their "yucky" pictures on their piece of cardboard labeled *yucky*.

The therapist asks the children, "Was there anything 'nice' about what happened?" If so, children can draw or find pictures to represent any positive aspects to their experience. These pictures are glued onto the other side of the cardboard labeled *nice*. Children then look through the magazines to find "nice" pictures or pictures of their favorite things. These are glued onto the cardboard side labeled *nice*. If desired, the therapist can give the child a scented sticker to glue on their collage of "nice" pictures.

Next, the therapist asks the children to look at their "yucky" pictures then their "nice" pictures and asks how they feel when they look at each picture. Children will likely give negative responses when looking at their "yucky" pictures and positive responses when looking at their "nice" pictures.

As a final step for this activity, children can be trained in visualization. The therapist asks the children to think of a nice thought and to practice thinking of that nice thought. The therapist can offer an example: "Close your eyes and picture a kitten. Imagine the feel of his soft, fluffy fur as you stroke his back. Imagine the sound of the kitten purring. Imagine the tickly feeling as the kitten licks your cheek with his tongue." The therapist ends by suggesting that the next time the children think of the secret touching, and it makes them feel "yucky," they can paractice visualizing and imagining their "nice picture" or their "nice thought" and this will help them to feel better.

DISCUSSION

It is difficult for young children to grasp the concept of triggers and even more complex for them to re-frame their negative reactions to triggers. This activity introduces young children to the concept of triggers indirectly by giving them a vocabulary to express things that make them feel "yucky." In addition, the activity provides young victims with a strategy to counter their negative reactions to triggers by helping them to think of positive thoughts. Because of the simplistic nature of this activity, desensitization exercises are recommended for children who are having stronger phobic reactions to triggers.

The therapist should keep in mind that it is especially important to help care givers understand the significance of this exercise and what it means to children (the early identification of possible future phobic responses).

Latency—Preteen
Memories

MODALITY: Individual, group

GOALS: To identify possible negative associations to the abuse experience; to gain an understanding of the relationship between sensory stimulation and memory; to prevent (by early identification) phobic reactions to triggers

MATERIALS

➤ Worksheet: "Memories" *following*

➤ "Strategy List" *following*

METHOD

ADVANCE PREPARATION:
The therapist copies the "Memories/Strategy" worksheet and list to distribute to the children.

ACTIVITY:
The therapist introduces the activity by asking each group member to describe a favorite memory. This leads nicely into a general discussion about memories and how some memories elicit positive feelings while other memories elicit negative feelings.

The therapist then explains that memories of sexual abuse may elicit no feelings, positive feelings, negative feelings, or mixed-up feelings. Negative feelings related to sexual victimization may vary in intensity— some memories may trigger a minor reaction, other memories may trigger a very strong phobic reaction.

The "Memories" worksheet is introduced as a way to help children identify their triggers. Once the worksheet has been completed, group members can brainstorm strategies to deal with strong negative reactions to memories. The leader can offer some suggestions, such as: draw a picture of the negative memory (to help desensitize); practice a relaxation exercise; refocus your thoughts on a happy memory.

DISCUSSION

In addition to enabling children to identify their triggers, this activity assists children in documenting significant memories. This is important, especially at the point of early intervention, because traumatized children often repress their memories in order to cope with the psychic pain of negative events. The second part of the activity encourages children to adopt safe coping strategies to deal with strong reactions to negative memories. Some of the activities from Chapter 4, "Coping With Feelings," may also be helpful in providing children with a repertoire of strategies to manage negative reactions to triggers.

WORKSHEET

MEMORIES

TOPIC	POSITIVE MEMORIES	NEGATIVE MEMORIES
PLACES		
PEOPLE		
SOUNDS		
SMELLS		
SIGHTS		
TASTES		
TOUCHES		
OTHER		

STRATEGY LIST

When I am experiencing a scary memory, I can:

Strategy #1: _____

Strategy #2: _____

Strategy #3: _____

Latency—Teen
Scene of the Crime

MODALITY: Individual, group

GOALS: To identify possible negative associations to the abuse experience; to gain an understanding of the relationship between sensory stimulation and memory; to prevent (by early identification) phobic reactions to triggers

MATERIALS

➤ Story: "Jennifer and Tommy" *following*

➤ Workbook: "Scene of the Crime" *following*

➤ Detective costumes (optional)

METHOD

ADVANCE PREPARATION:
Copy the workbook pages for children to use in this activity.

ACTIVITY:
The therapist introduces the concept of triggers by reading the story about Jennifer and Tommy. The story is then discussed in terms of how certain things reminded Jennifer and Tommy of the sexual abuse and how these reminders continued to make them feel awful even after the sexual abuse had stopped.

The therapist then leads into the activity by explaining: "It is common for certain things to remind victims of the sexual abuse. These reminders can cause negative or uncomfortable reactions. For example, when you see someone who looks like the abuser, you may react by feeling scared or anxious. This activity will help you identify the things that remind you of the sexual abuse, and will teach you what to do when you have an uncomfortable or scary reaction to these reminders."

The therapist provides each child with a "Scene of the Crime" workbook. As the children complete their workbooks, the therapist can ask "prompt" questions, such as:

- What was the room like?
- What color were the walls?
- What noises did you hear?
- What did the blanket on the bed feel like?
- What did the abuser look like?
- What was the abuser wearing?
- Did the abuser smoke or drink?

DISCUSSION

This activity helps sexual abuse victims to first label their triggers and then identify alternate thoughts, so they are better able to cope with these triggers. In using this activity, the therapist should note that sexual victims will be negatively triggered to varying degrees and not all victims will be triggered by things from all the five senses.

The activity is purposely called "Scene of the Crime" to help children view themselves as victims and abusers as perpetrators of a criminal act. This is important as children's sense of guilt will be reduced if they are able to see that a crime was committed against them.

JENNIFER AND TOMMY

Jennifer and Tommy are twins. They're not identical twins because one is a boy and one is a girl.

They're both terrific kids. They love TV and going to McDonald's. As for school, their favorite subjects are recess and gym. Jennifer is good at math and Tommy likes to read.

For a long time they had a secret they were both afraid to share. The secret finally came out. Their Uncle Max sexually abused them almost every time he was asked to baby-sit. After each of the twins found out that Uncle Max was touching both of them, they talked it over and decided to tell their parents. Tommy told their mom and then told Jen to tell their dad.

That was very hard to do. Things were unsettled for quite some time. The whole family went for help.

Certain things reminded Jennifer of Uncle Max. He smoked cigars; so whenever she smelled cigar smoke, Jennifer's heart started to pound. She worked up her courage to tell her brother. "The same with me!" blurted Tommy, "Whenever anyone asks me if I want a chocolate bar, I think about how he bribed me with Snickers bars. I hate them now!"

Uncle Max would always try to touch Jennifer when she was changing into her p.j.'s. She hated the sight of them now. They had a koala bear on the knee and a bunch of balloons on the pocket. Tommy remembered that Uncle Max used to say things to him. Things like, "You're special, TomBo." Some of his friends at school called him Tombo.

The twins decided to ask for help. They were pretty mad that Uncle Max had touched them. And that's not all — he'd ruined Snickers bars and balloon pajamas and lots of other things.

WORKBOOK

SCENE

OF THE

CRIME

Think back to the scene of the crime—where the sexual abuse happened. If the sexual abuse happened more than once, then think back to one particular time. Use one of the pictures or draw the place where the sexual abuse happened. (This may be a room in a house, an outdoor area like a park, or somewhere else like a car.) Include yourself and the abuser in the picture.

Look at the picture of the scene of the crime and answer the following questions:

What do you <u>see</u> at the scene of the crime? _____

_____

_____

What does the scene of the crime <u>smell</u> like? _____

_____

_____

What do you <u>taste</u> at the scene of the crime? _____

_____

_____

What do you <u>touch</u> at the scene of the crime? _____

_____

_____

What do you <u>hear</u> at the scene of the crime? _____

_____

_____

When you see, smell, taste, touch or hear something that reminds you of the sexual abuse and you get a scary or anxious reaction, you can think of something nice instead. For example, when you smell cigarette smoke and it reminds you of the abuser's breath, you can think of smelling a fresh batch of chocolate chip cookies instead! You can begin to make a list of these things, so next time you get a reaction, you will be prepared!

When I **see** _____ I remember _____ .

When this happens, I can think of seeing _____

instead, because this will help me.

When I **smell** _____ I remember _____ .

When this happens, I can think of smelling _____

instead, because this will help me.

When I **taste** _____ I remember _____ .

When this happens I can think of tasting _____

instead, because this will help me.

When I **touch** _____ I remember _____ .

When this happens I can think of touching _____

instead, because this will help me.

When I **hear** ____ I remember .

When this happens I can think of hearing _____

instead, because this will help me.

PAPER DOLLS AND PAPER AIRPLANES

Latency—Teen
Reminders

MODALITY: Individual, group

GOALS: To identify possible negative associations to the abuse experience; to gain an understanding of the relationship between sensory stimulation and memory; to prevent (by early identification) phobic reactions to triggers

MATERIALS

➤ 4 sandwich bags

➤ Various items to fill bags (see Method Section)

➤ Full-color fashion magazines and department store catalogs

➤ Scissors

➤ Glue sticks

➤ Markers and crayons

➤ Booklet: "Things That Remind Me of the Sexual Abuse" *following*

➤ Handout: Dealing With Triggers *following*

METHOD

ADVANCE PREPARATION:

The therapist makes a copy of the booklets for each child then makes four bags:

1) a "feel bag" by filling a sandwich bag with various items with different textures, such as a cotton ball, sandpaper, an orange rind.
2) a "smell bag" with items such as an onion, perfume, baby powder.
3) a "taste bag" with samples of lemon, jam, salted crackers.
4) a "sound bag" with various objects such as a bell, a drum, a whistle.

ACTIVITY:

The therapist begins by asking the children if they know the different senses (see, smell, taste, touch, hear). The leader then introduces the bags by saying: "When we touch or smell or taste or hear something, our body reacts." The children close their eyes and the items in the bags are passed around the group for the children to touch, smell, taste, and listen to. Children can describe the body sensations and reactions as they handle the items. Children will enjoy the suspense as the mystery items are passed around.

The therapist then states: "It is normal for the body to react when it sees or smells or tastes or touches or hears something. Sometimes the body reacts in a nice way, like if we see or smell a beautiful flower. Other times the body reacts in a yucky way like if we smell a poopy diaper!" At this point the children can be encouraged to give their own examples of things they see, smell, taste, touch, or hear and tell about how their body reacts.

The therapist then states: "When children are sexually abused, there are often things that they see or smell or taste or touch or hear that remind them of the sexual abuse. Like if your abuser smoked, then seeing a pack of cigarettes or smelling cigarette smoke may remind you of the sexual abuse." Children are then asked to think back to the sexual abuse, and to write down or draw the things that remind them of the sexual abuse and to describe their reactions to these triggers. They can look through the magazines and cut out pictures of things that remind them of the abuse. Children can paste these pictures and words into the corresponding places in their booklets. For example, "Things I see..." refers to anything the child sees that is a reminder of the abuse, such as a picture of a bed; or if the abuser bribed the child with candy, then the child can place a candy wrapper in the space titled "Things I Taste..."

Children develop positive re-frames for each trigger item that they have placed in their booklet. For instance, if a bed was listed as a trigger, it can be re-framed as follows: Beds are good to sleep in and to hear a bedtime story. The therapist can explain to the child that the next time the child sees a bed and begins to feel scared or anxious, he/she can think of a favorite bedtime story. Another way to neutralize a trigger is to make the trigger seem less scary by helping the child to visualize the trigger differently. For example, "Think of your bed with Mickey Mouse sheets on it!" Children may need help from the therapist to develop appropriate re-frames.

For older children, the handout "Dealing with Triggers" can be read aloud and discussed. Copies can be given to group members to take home.

DISCUSSION

This activity aims to help sexually abused children identify negative triggers, become desensitized and develop positive re-frames. Some sexual abuse victims will have stronger reactions to stimuli and will need more time during therapy to counter their phobias.

This activity was developed for the Crisis Support Group Program at the Metropolitan Toronto Special Committee on Child Abuse and is being used with their permission.

BOOKLET

THINGS THAT REMIND ME OF THE SEXUAL ABUSE

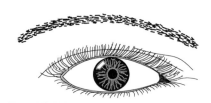

THINGS I SEE THAT REMIND ME OF SEXUAL ABUSE...

THINGS I SMELL THAT REMIND ME OF SEXUAL ABUSE...

THINGS I **HEAR** THAT REMIND ME OF SEXUAL ABUSE...

THINGS I TASTE THAT REMIND ME OF SEXUAL ABUSE...

THINGS I TOUCH THAT REMIND ME OF SEXUAL ABUSE...

REFRAME

_____ are good for:

<u>**HANDOUT**</u>

DEALING WITH TRIGGERS

Many triggers are natural aspects of ordinary life. They occur frequently and are not easily avoided. Some triggers are directly related to sexual behavior, or physical or emotional intimacy. To a sexual abuse victim, sudden, seemingly irrational fears can result in feelings of panic and out-of-control terror.

PLAN

Whenever you experience a negative association and uncomfortable reaction, try to acknowledge what is actually happening. Whenever the surge of panic hits, say to yourself, "Stop!" This is hard to do because automatic reactions can happen very fast and take you by complete surprise. Try to become aware of what triggered your reaction. If you cannot make the connection at the time, write down the details of the incident while it is still fresh in your memory.

A relaxation plan involves the following steps:

1) Check for signs— are you fearful or panicky? Are you sexually aroused? Are you panting? Are you sweating? Is your heart racing?

2) Breathe slowly, deeply. Place your hand over your heart and slowly talk to your heart—*slower, slower*.

3) Slowly clench and relax your fists.

4) Notice and describe who you are and where you are. For example, you might say, "I'm Jennifer. I'm 14, I'm not six. I'm at the cottage with friends. It's sunny. I'm safe. No one can hurt me."

5) Deal with the trigger. Decide to:
   a) remove yourself
   b) alter the trigger
   c) approach the trigger slowly
   d) accept the trigger
   e) alter your response.

Latency—Teen
Trigger Box Game

MODALITY: Individual, group

GOALS: To identify possible negative associations to the abuse experience; to gain an understanding of the relationship between sensory stimulation and memory; to prevent (by early identification) phobic reactions to triggers

MATERIALS

➤ "Trigger Box" filled with items *following*

➤ Situation Cards *following*

➤ Large construction paper sheets or mural paper folded in half (one per group member)

➤ Magazine pictures

➤ Glue

➤ Scissors

PAPER DOLLS AND PAPER AIRPLANES

METHOD

ADVANCE PREPARATION:

The therapist labels the outside of a box *Trigger Box*. It is then filled with the various things listed in the "Trigger Box Items" sheet. The Situation Cards are cut out (if desired, they can be mounted onto cardboard for extra durability).

ACTIVITY:

The leader begins the activity by drawing items, one at a time, out of the trigger box. As each item is pulled from the box, group members are provided with an opportunity to describe any reactions they have to it. The items are displayed on a table that is visible to all group members.

The Situation Cards are then distributed to the group members. Group members take turns reading the card aloud to the group, identifying the trigger in the situation, and matching the situation with the appropriate item from the Trigger Box that is displayed on the table. This game leads nicely into a discussion of the relationship between sensory stimulation and memory activation.

The next part of the activity involves a two-step collage. The leader provides each group member with a large sheet of paper that is folded in half. On the left side of the paper, children are to make a collage to represent "Memories, Reminders and Triggers Related to the Sexual Abuse." On the right side, a collage is created to illustrate "Places, People and Things That Make Me Feel Safe." Magazine pictures, actual items, and other materials can be used to make the collages.

DISCUSSION

Phobic reactions to triggers are a part of a child's legacy of sexual abuse. To a sexual abuse victim, sudden, seemingly irrational fears can result in feelings of panic and out-of-control terror. A crucial step in the recovery process for sexually abused children is to help them to identify their triggers, and to prevent ongoing phobic reactions. This activity helps to neutralize triggers and ultimately gives sexual victims a sense of power and control.

Note: This activity should be used following an activity in which children have already had an opportunity to identify their individual triggers.

SITUATION CARDS

Allison was abused by her uncle. She still remembers the smell of his aftershave lotion.	Jesse was abused by an older boy. The older boy smoked cigarettes and he offered "smokes" to Jesse.
Stan was always abused by his older brother on Saturday mornings while they were watching cartoons on television.	Sally was building sand castles at the beach when an older man asked her to come see some really neat seaweed. He sexually abused her in a private cove where nobody could see.
Carmen was really scared when she saw white stuff squirt out of the abuser's penis.	Amanda thought about the sexual abuse whenever she got her period.
Robert was abused by his older sister when she was giving him a bath.	Patty's father was always drunk when he sexually abused her.
Danny was abused by the guy at the doughnut shop. The abuser had lots of tattoos on his arms.	Kimisha was asked to pose naked while the abuser took pictures of her.

ITEMS FOR TRIGGER BOX

(Place the following items or magazine pictures of the following items in the Trigger Box)

➤ After shave lotion

➤ Cigarettes

➤ Comic Strips

➤ Sea shell

➤ Hair Styling Mousse that comes out in a foam

➤ Tampon

➤ Picture of a bathtub

➤ Liquor bottle

➤ Tattoo/decals

➤ Camera

Chapter 11
Sexuality

PURPOSE OF THE CHAPTER:

Sexual abuse prematurely introduces children to sexual activity. It disrupts and interferes with the normative process of sexual development. How this disruption will affect children will be seen at various points in their future development. Some of the signs of issues in the sexual development area are: negative body image, negative attitudes toward sexual material, confusion about touch (i.e. safe vs. unsafe touch), avoidance and/or boundary issues.

The activities in this chapter are designed to provide a beginning framework for understanding sexuality as a healthy part of development and to separate the sexual abuse experience from the child's basic comfort level with his/her sexuality. These activities are both present-focused (redefining the child's current perception of his/her sexuality) and future-focused (providing building blocks for future sexual development).

It is important that care givers are informed and knowledgeable about these activities. The parent-child model of providing service is especially important for this component. Parents' comfort level, knowledge-base, and understanding of these concepts as they relate to their child's future is critical to maximizing the effectiveness of this work.

The authors acknowledge that issues regarding sexuality are lifelong and developmentally based. As children proceed through their development, unresolved issues will resurface for reworking. The activities in this chapter are meant to provide a framework from which to begin this work and to increase the child's comfort level with the issue of sexuality.

Preschool
Dress-Up

MODALITY: Individual, group

GOAL: To teach body awareness and to reinforce the concept of private body parts

MATERIALS

➤ Body Outlines *following*

➤ Dress-up clothes *following*

➤ Scissors

➤ Glue sticks

➤ 2 garbage bags each filled with an assortment of adult clothing

METHOD

ADVANCE PREPARATION:
Collect the items needed for this activity and make copies of the body outlines and clothes pages for each group member.

ACTIVITY:
The group leader provides each child with one set of paper dress up clothes and five paper body outlines (baby, boy, girl, man, woman). Children are to select which clothing item belongs to each paper doll.

Care givers then cut out the paper clothes and the children can "dress up" the dolls by gluing the paper clothes onto the appropriate paper dolls. (Anatomical dolls can be used as an alternative.) This activity leads nicely into a discussion of the following questions:

- What names do kids use for the private body parts and what are the correct names for these body parts?
- How are boys and girls different?
- How are children and adults different?
- How are private body parts different from other body parts?
- When is it OK for someone to touch your private body parts?

The second part of the activity involves a "dress-up relay race." The children are divided into two groups. Each group is provided with a garbage bag filled with various items of adult clothing, such as slacks, shirt, hat, shoes, etc. One person from each group starts the race by putting on all the clothes from the bag, running to the other end of the room, running back to the group, taking off the clothes and giving them to the next person in line. The first group to have all the players complete the relay wins!

DISCUSSION

Through this activity, children will learn about their bodies and how their bodies are different from the opposite sex and from adults. The activity provides the forum to address appropriate sexual boundaries such as, "We don't go to the supermarket naked," and "We don't touch anybody else's private parts." Jan Hindman's *A Very Touching Book* is a good companion to this activity. The children can participate in various songs and games that reinforce the concept of body awareness, such as "The Hokey Pokey" and "Simon Says."

DRESS-UP CLOTHES

BODY OUTLINES

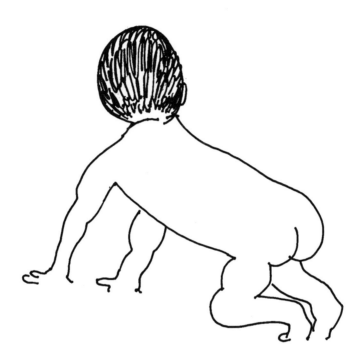

BODY OUTLINE

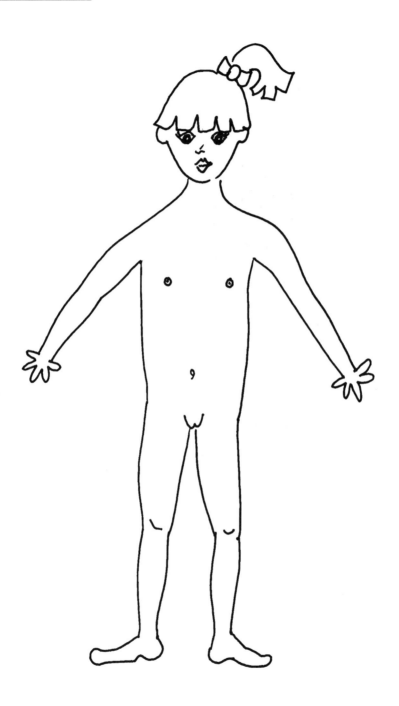

BODY OUTLINE

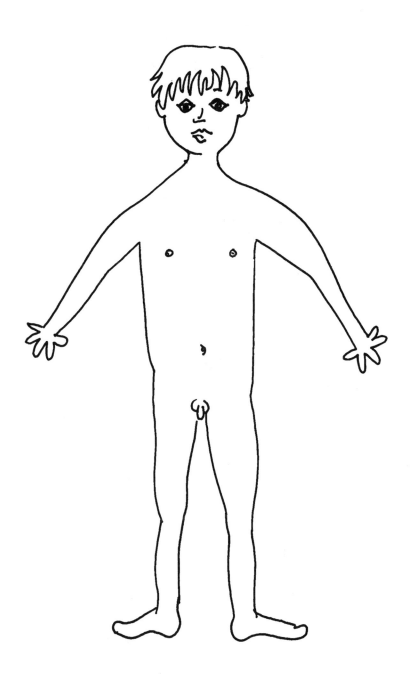

PAPER DOLLS AND PAPER AIRPLANES

BODY OUTLINES

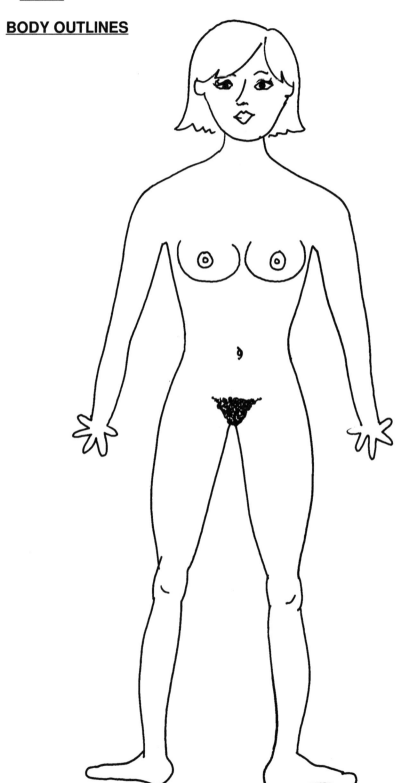

372

BODY OUTLINES

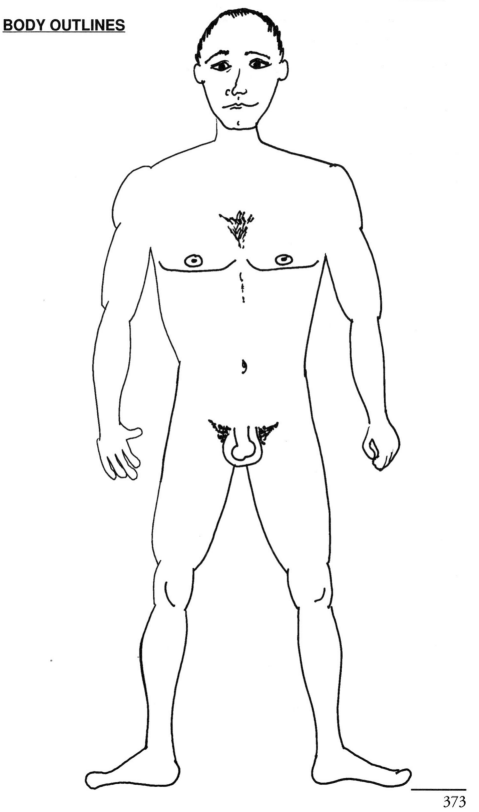

Preschool—Latency
Touch I Like to Give and Get

MODALITY: Individual, group

GOALS: To acknowledge the value of positive touch; to encourage children to ask for and receive positive touch; to encourage children to demonstrate their feelings of caring and affection in appropriate ways

MATERIAL

➤ Touch Pictures *following*

➤ Crayons, markers

➤ Scissors

➤ Glue

➤ Magazines

➤ Stickers

METHOD

ADVANCE PREPARATION:
Make copies of the Touch Pictures to pass out to the children.

ACTIVITY:
The group brainstorms to put together a list of positive touches. Care givers, children, and leaders are encouraged to contribute to a list.

For example:

kisses	finger painting
hugs	making cookies
cuddles	rocking a baby
squeezes	cuddling a puppy
bear hugs	taking a bubble bath
pats on the back	having a cold shower
burping a baby	slap on the back
a back tickle	arm wrestling
someone brushing your hair	foot massage
pillow fight	high-five
making mud pies	cuddling a stuffed toy
holding hands with a friend	squirting a friend with a water pistol
putting an ice cube down someone's back	
having a snowball fight	

Children can then look at the Touch Pictures with their care givers and circle with one color crayon "Touch I Like to Give" and with another color, "Touch I Like to Get."

The last part of this activity consists of giving each child an opportunity to share a collection of good touches with the group.

DISCUSSION

Young children who have been sexually abused need opportunities to receive and express physical affection in appropriate ways. They benefit from acknowledging the need for pleasurable, safe touch and will require help learning to ask for touch.

This activity offers an excellent opportunity to introduce the theme of privacy and the right to say "no" to any kind of touch. Children will enjoy the story of "King Midas," which fits nicely into this theme.

TOUCH PICTURES

Kisses

hugs

squeezes

bear hug

cuddles

pat on the back

burping a baby

back tickle

Someone brushing your hair

having a pillow fight

PAPER DOLLS AND PAPER AIRPLANES

making mud pies

holding hands with a friend

putting an icecube down someone's back

finger painting

having a snowball fight

making cookies

squirting a friend with a water pistol

rocking a baby

cuddling a puppy

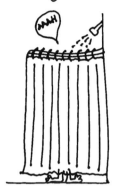
having a cold shower

AAAH

having a bubble bath

A slap on the back

arm wrestling

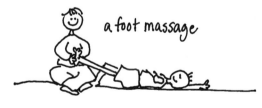
a foot massage

cuddling a stuffed toy

high five

Latency—Teen
Match Game

MODALITY: Individual, group

GOAL: To teach children correct definitions of sexual terms

MATERIALS

➤ Worksheet: "Match Game" *following*

➤ Pencils

➤ Glossary

METHOD

ADVANCE PREPARATION:
The therapist will make copies of the worksheet to distribute for this activity.

ACTIVITY:
Children complete the "Match Game" worksheet by reading the words on the left and connecting them to their appropriate definitions on the right. The therapist then reads the glossary aloud while the children check to see if their answers are correct.

DISCUSSION

Children have a tendency to become bored and/or embarrassed in the face of a sex education lesson. The "Match Game" is a more appealing way to provide children with a vocabulary of key sexual terms.

MATCH GAME

Draw a line to connect each word on the left with its appropriate definition on the right:

Puberty	When a male has sexual fantasies while sleeping and ejaculates
Ejaculation	Acquired Immune Deficiency Syndrome; a deadly disease you can get through the exchange of infected body fluids, contaminated needles, a tainted blood transfusion
Tampon	Piece of skin at the opening of the vagina which can be broken by sexual or other physical contact
Clitoris	When the body begins to change and a person becomes capable of sexual reproduction
Wet dream	When the penis discharges semen
Masturbation	A cotton plug inserted into the vagina to absorb blood during a period
AIDS	Very sensitive part of the vagina that feels good when rubbed
Hymen	When a person becomes sexually excited to the point of climax
Orgasm	Birth control
Contraception	Touching one's own sexual organs

GLOSSARY OF SEXUAL TERMS

Puberty .... when the body begins to change and a person becomes capable of sexual reproduction

Ejaculation .... when the penis discharges semen

Tampon .... a cotton plug inserted into the vagina to absorb blood during a period

Clitoris .... very sensitive part of the vagina that feels good when rubbed

Wet dream .... when a male has sexual fantasies while sleeping and ejaculates

Masturbation ..... touching one's own sexual organs

AIDS .... Acquired Immune Deficiency Syndrome; a deadly disease you can get through the exchange of infected body fluids, contaminated needles, a tainted blood transfusion

Hymen .... piece of skin at the opening of the vagina which can be broken by sexual or other physical contact

Orgasm .... when a person becomes sexually excited to the point of climax

Contraception ... birth control

Latency—Teen
The Sex Game

MODALITY: Group

GOAL: To help children become more comfortable discussing sexual issues and to teach sex education

MATERIALS

➤ Colored index cards or cardboard (white, blue, green, and yellow)

➤ Spinner (paper plate and popsicle stick attached with thumb tack) *following*

METHOD

ADVANCE PREPARATION:
The group leader writes the "Sex Game" questions onto colored cardboard. Questions are divided into three categories: *sex trivia*, *body parts*, and *relationships*. A different color card is used for each category (blue cards for sex trivia; green cards for body parts; yellow cards for relationships). A spinner is made by copying the Spinner outline onto a paper plate or piece of cardboard, and a popsicle stick is pinned to the center. Note that the "Sex Game" question cards can be adapted to fit the particular age group of the children.

ACTIVITY:

The "Sex Game" is explained to the group as follows: "Players take turns spinning the wheel. The spinner lands on a space that corresponds to a stack of cards: *sex trivia*, *body parts*, and *relationships*. If the spinner lands on *Free Choice*, then the player can choose from any one of the three categories. Once a question card is selected, the player can answer the question, pass, or ask the group for help in answering the question.

DISCUSSION

Talking about sexuality can be anxiety-provoking, particularly for sexual abuse victims. The game format provides a less threatening modality to help children learn and talk about sex-related issues. Question cards can be used to elicit further discussion. The therapist should become familiar with the question cards and be prepared for any discussion or issues that arise during the game. The group leader should also be prepared to deal with the children's anxiety. If group members become giddy, the therapist can label and normalize this behavior. The therapist should also be aware of his/her own comfort level with respect to discussing sexual issues, because the group will sense if the therapist is embarrassed. It is extremely important that the therapist does not judge or impose his/her own value system. Rather, the therapist should create a comfortable atmosphere that encourages openness and sharing.

Group members will exhibit varied knowledge of human sexuality. Some children will have received sex education at school or from their parents while other children will have little information. The more knowledgeable group members can be encouraged to take on a leadership role during the game. If using the game with latency aged children, it may be helpful to begin the session by showing a video or reading a book about human sexuality (see resource section).

SEX GAME QUESTION CARDS

SEX TRIVIA

1) How are babies made?

2) What is puberty?

3) How do you go about having sexual intercourse?

4) What is masturbation? If your parents find you masturbating, should they punish you?

5) What is an orgasm? How do you know if you have one?

6) What is a contraceptive? Can you name two kinds of contraceptives?

7) True or False: A girl can use her friend's birth control pills.

8) What is an S.T.D.? Can you name two?

9) What is foreplay?

10) What is a pelvic exam?

11) True or False: A girl can get pregnant the first time she has sexual intercourse.

12) What does *safe sex* mean?

13) What is a wet dream?

14) Do all girls bleed and have pain the first time they have sexual intercourse?

15) What is the difference between fellatio and cunnilingus?

16) What is AIDS? How do you get AIDS?

17) True or False: Every vagina looks exactly the same.

18) Can a woman get pregnant if she has sex during her period?

19) What is the difference between a heterosexual, a homosexual, and a bisexual?

20) What is a lubricant and where can you get it?

21) What is a tampon? What is a sanitary napkin?

22) True or False: You can start the pill anytime and it will be effective right away.

23) What is the difference between a hand job and a blow job?

24) What is a vibrator?

25) What is a French kiss?

BODY PARTS

1) Name three parts of the penis.
2) Name three parts of the vagina.
3) What is the vulva?
4) What are three things that happen to a boy's body during puberty?
5) What are three things that happen to a girl's body during puberty?
6) What is it called when blood comes out of the woman's vagina each month?
7) In a woman's vaginal area, how many holes, or openings are there?
8) Name three places where hair grows on a woman's or man's body during puberty
9) True or False: A big penis makes more babies than a small penis.
10) Do both men and women have breasts?
11) In what part of the female's body does a baby develop?
12) What is the urethra?
13) What is an erection? How often and when do boys have them?
14) What is impotence?
15) True or false: Boys often wake up in the morning with an erection.
16) What are vaginal secretions?
17) True or False: You should go see a doctor if sores develop on your penis or vagina.
18) What comes out of the penis during ejaculation?
19) True or false: The bigger the penis, the more satisfying it is for a woman during sexual intercourse.
20) What is a clitoris?
21) What is a hymen?
22) On a woman's breasts, what happens to the nipples when they are touched?
23) What are scrotum?
24) True or False: Certain exercises make a woman's breasts larger.
25) Does the penis grow bigger as it is used more?

RELATIONSHIPS

1) Do you feel pressure to have a boy friend or girl friend?

2) Should a boy and girl kiss on a first date?

3) What should you do if you start to think about the sexual abuse while you are with a boy friend or girl friend?

4) How do you feel if you are at a party and nobody asks you to dance?

5) What do you have to offer in a relationship?

6) What would you do if you saw your best friend's boy friend or girl friend treating your friend badly?

7) Do you think it is OK for a girl to ask a boy out on a date?

8) What should a person do if a boy bragged to his friends that he had sex with a girl when he really didn't?

9) What would you do if your boyfriend asked you to go on the pill?

10) What would you do if your girl friend asked you to wear a condom during sexual intercourse?

11) How often should people have sex?

12) What would you do if you had a boy friend or girl friend and you met someone else you really liked?

13) What would you do if your boy friend refused to wear a condom during sex?

14) What would you do if you and your partner got into a fight and your partner hit you?

15) What do you think is the most important thing in a relationship?

16) What would the man or woman of your dreams be like?

17) How can a girl stop a boy when she doesn't want to go any farther sexually?

18) When is it OK for two people to have sexual intercourse for the first time?

19) What is rape? Is it possible for a husband to rape his wife?

20) How do you put on a condom?

21) Do you think it is OK for people to "make out" in front of other people?

22) How do you know if the person you are dating has a venereal disease?

23) What is your opinion of premarital sex?

24) What would you do if you caught your girl friend or boy friend kissing someone else?

25) How do you know if you are in love?

PAPER DOLLS AND PAPER AIRPLANES

SPINNER FOR THE SEX GAME

Copy the outline below on a paper plate or piece of cardboard and attach a spinner to the center.

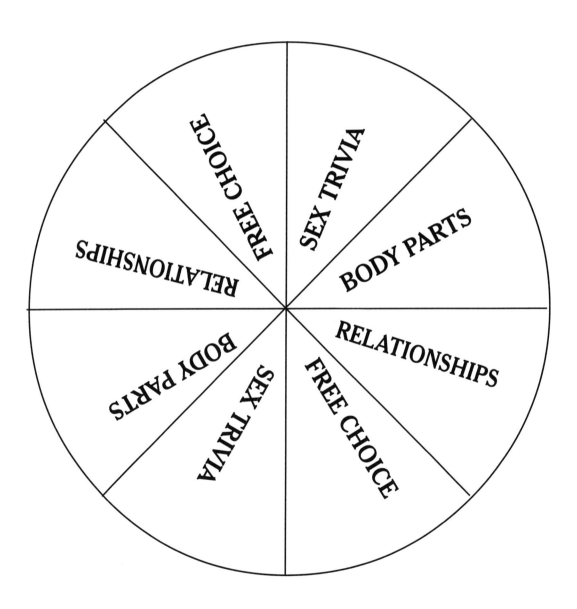

Preteen
Puberty Kit

MODALITY: Individual, group

GOAL: To provide pre-pubescent children with accurate information about sexual development and reproduction

MATERIALS

➤ Shoe box

➤ Handout: "The Preteen's Guide to Puberty" *following*

➤ Puberty Kit items: razor, deodorant, sanitary napkin, tampon, bra

METHOD

ADVANCE PREPARATION:

The "Puberty Kit" is prepared by filling a shoe box with the following items: copies of "The Preteen's Guide to Puberty" for each group member, a razor, a stick or roll-on deodorant, a bra, a sanitary napkin, and a tampon.

ACTIVITY:

The leader begins by asking the group, "Who knows what puberty means?" The group members are given an opportunity to provide definitions. The leader then opens the Puberty Kit and begins by distributing "The Preteen's Guide to Puberty" handout to the group. The group reads through the handout and the leader encourages discussion. Various props are included in the Puberty Kit for the leader to show the group during the discussion. For example, the sanitary napkin and tampon can be displayed when the group is talking about menstruation.

The leader should leave ample time for the girls to ask questions and to talk about their feelings related to the onset of puberty. The leader may wish to add other items to the Puberty Kit, such as acne cream or a teen "heart throb" magazine. Humor is encouraged to diminish the group's anxiety about the topic!

DISCUSSION

Many children receive inaccurate information about sexuality and puberty. This activity provides preteens with important information about issues of concern. The leader should strive to create an atmosphere that encourages open discussion. If the group members seem hesitant to ask questions, the leader can provide the group with a question box so that they can put forth their questions anonymously.

The therapist should recognize that knowledge about sexual issues, emotional maturity and sexual experiences will differ among group members. Moreover, cultural and religious beliefs about sexual issues vary and should be respected.

Helpful resources on this topic include: "The Growing Up Series," a video available from The National Film Board Of Canada and the following books: *Asking About Sex and Growing Up* by Joanna Cole (Morrow Junior Books, 1988) and *Changing Bodies, Changing Lives* by Ruth Bell, et al. (Vintage, 1987).

HANDOUT

THE PRETEEN'S GUIDE TO PUBERTY

Q: *What is puberty?*
A: Puberty is a time when the body goes through changes and become capable of sexual reproduction.

Q: *What changes does a girl go through during puberty?*
A: Her body shape changes (her breasts get larger, her hips get wider and her waist narrows); she starts to grow hair on her legs, under her arms, and around her crotch (this is called pubic hair); she begins to menstruate (get her period) and her sex organs grow (her uterus gets larger, the ovaries grow and begin to get ready for releasing egg cells, and her vagina and clitoris get larger). These changes happen for different girls at different times, but most girls have reached puberty by their mid-teens.

Q: *What changes does a boy go through during puberty?*
A: His body starts to change (he grows taller; his shoulders get broader; his muscles get larger; he may develop small bumps under his nipples); he starts to grow hair on his face, under his arms, on his legs, and around his penis (this is called pubic hair); his sex organs grow (his testicles become larger and hang lower, his penis grows larger and becomes slightly darker, he begins to produce sperm that can combine with an egg cell in a woman's body to make a baby); he begins to have wet dreams (he ejaculates during sleep, often after having a sexy dream); and his voice gets deeper.

Q: *Why do girls have periods? What is a period like? What should a girl do about it?*
A: Menstruation (getting a period) happens when the female's

body is getting ready to have a baby. The lining of the uterus gets thicker with nourishing blood. If the woman is not pregnant, the lining flows out of the uterus and through the vagina. Girls discover they have begun their period when they notice a brownish-red stain on their underwear. They may have physical symptoms like stomach cramps or headaches. A period usually comes 28 to 30 days, but for some girls, it may be irregular. It lasts for three to seven days. Girls start their periods anywhere from age nine to 15. There are two products a girl can use to absorb the menstrual blood. A sanitary napkin, or pad, which has an adhesive strip on one side to stick to the crotch of the underpants, or a tampon, a cotton plug which is inserted into the vagina. Both of these products are available at drugstores. Getting a period may be uncomfortable, but there are things girls can do to feel better, such as taking medication or having a soothing bath. Menstruation is a normal part of growing up for girls and it is the start of the wonderful process of becoming a woman!

Q: *What are sperm? What are ejaculations? When does this start for boys?*

A: Sperm are cells that are produced in the testicles (the two oval shaped organs on each side of the penis). A male's body makes sperm so the cells can combine with a woman's egg to create a baby. Sperm are so small they can only be seen through a microscope. Boy's begin to produce sperm when they are between the ages of 11 and 15. Once a boy's body begins to make sperm, he will start having ejaculations (the penis gets hard and a thick, white liquid called *semen* comes out of the penis). The sperm cells are mixed in the semen. Boys usually ejaculate when they masturbate (rub their penis for pleasure) or when they have a wet dream (a sexy dream). Masturbating, having wet dreams, and ejaculations are a normal part of growing up for boys!

Source: *Asking About Sex & Growing Up* by Joanna Cole, New York: Morrow Junior Books,1988.

Teen
Pressure Points

MODALITY: Individual, group

GOALS: To gain skills in evaluating relationships; to develop assertiveness skills related to decisions about sexual expression

MATERIALS:

➤ Worksheet: "Rate Your Relationships" *following*

➤ Pins

➤ Flip chart or chalkboard

MATERIALS

ADVANCE PREPARATION:
Make copies of the worksheet to use during this activity.

ACTIVITY:
The therapist begins the activity by having the group brainstorm a list of qualities they value in a relationship, for example:

- Trust
- Communication
- Loyalty
- Sensitivity

- Sense Of Humor
- Caring
- Loving
- Responsible

The therapist then distributes the worksheet. On completion, the therapist leads a discussion about what group members learned about themselves and their relationships.

The next part of the activity consists of going over the stages of expression of physical touch with the group:

1. smiles and encouragement
2. hugs
3. arms around each other
4. kissing
5. exploring above waist
6. exploring below waist
7. sexual intercourse.

This list can be written on a chalkboard or flip chart. As the list is developed, bodily reactions are described.

The final part of this activity reinforces that girls (and boys) can say "no" to any stage of sexual expression. Practice is given then by having the group come up with a list of responses to pressure lines, for example:

"You had sex with me last week—what's the big deal?"

"Come on! Everybody's doing it!"

"I won't go out with you anymore if we don't do it."

"I'll tell everybody you did, if you refuse!"

DISCUSSION

Healthy sexual development, positive attitudes about sexuality and intimate relationships are typically affected by sexual abuse. In particular, puberty, marriage, pregnancy and childbirth are key developmental milestones that often present a challenge to the sexual abuse survivors.

An important aspect of treatment is providing the knowledge and skills to help youth resolve these developmental crises.

The first part of this activity helps young people identify the qualities they value in relationships.

The second part of the activity helps to reassure the young people about comfort levels in progressive expressions of sexual feelings. It is an opportunity to confirm the right of any person to say "no" at any stage of sexual activity.

RATE YOUR RELATIONSHIPS

Values	Person of the Same Sex	Person of the Opposite Sex	Older Person Either Sex	Self
1.				
2.				
3.				
4.				
5.				

RATING SCALE:
0 = Does not have this quality at all
1 = Has this quality in a few instances
2 = Has this quality but not all the time
3 = Shows this quality consistently

RATE YOUR RELATIONSHIPS
In the first column list five qualities that are important to you in a personal relationship. At the top of the next column write the initials of a person of the same sex with whom you have an important relationship. On the next column write the initials of someone of the opposite sex. On the fourth column, write the initials of an older person, male or female. On the last column write your initials. Now rate yourself and others by using the rating scale. Add up the scores for the 5 qualities (a perfect score = 20).

Chapter 12
Personal Safety

PURPOSE OF THE CHAPTER:
Re-victimization rates for children with sexual abuse histories are quite high (Briere, Runtz, 1988). It is hoped that through a comprehensive trauma assessment, children's vulnerabilities will be adequately determined, enabling the development of effective treatment modalities to address these vulnerabilities. This manual can serve as part of that therapeutic intervention.

The personal safety chapter offers a number of activities providing both cognitive and experiential opportunities to assist children in understanding personal safety concepts and how they work.

It is not the intention of the authors to suggest that the successful completion of these activities will result in an assurance that future re-victimization will not occur. There are many factors that contribute to re-victimization, including parental supervision, unsafe environments, and the determination and skill of child molesters.

Enhancing children's awareness, knowledge, and skills in this area is an important component to personal safety, but clearly only one of many components. Further, the authors wish to emphasize that it is not the responsibility of children to protect themselves. Rather, it is the responsibility of adults (parents, care givers, and the community at large) to provide safe, protective, and nurturing environments in which children can be raised.

Preschool—Latency

The OK to Say No Game

MODALITY: Group

GOAL: To prevent further sexual victimization by teaching children about situations that may be potentially abusive and to reinforce appropriate assertiveness skills

M A T E R I A L S

➤ "OK to Say No" game board *following*

➤ Poster board

➤ Index cards or cardboard

➤ Happy face stickers (one per child)

M E T H O D

ADVANCE PREPARATION:

The therapist copies the "OK to Say No" game board onto a larger piece of poster board or colored cardboard. Game cards are made using index cards or cardboard cut into squares. The cards are numbered from *1* to *15*. Four cards are reserved for "surprise cards." Each of the following surprise statements are written on a separate card:

1) It's OK to say "NO" to secret touching! Practice yelling "NO!" as loud as you can!

2) It's OK to say "YES!" to good touching! Ask someone in the group for a hug!

3) You are learning to take good care of yourself! Give yourself a hug!

4) Your body is special! Take a happy face sticker and give one to each person in the group.

ACTIVITY:

The leader introduces the activity by saying "Sometimes it's OK for you to say no—if someone is hurting you, it's OK to say 'NO!' to put a stop to it. But other times, it's not OK to say 'NO!'—if your parents tell you to do something that is for your own good. We're going to play a game that will help us understand when it is OK for kids to say no. (*The leader places the game board on the floor with the children sitting around it.*) To play this game, we will take turns picking a card with a number on it and reading the situation on the game board with that same number. When the situation is read aloud, you must decide if it is okay or not okay to say no for that situation. For example, for situation #2: 'A stranger asks you to come see his puppy.' It is okay to say no, because you should never go with a stranger because you may get hurt!" (*If this activity is being used with preschoolers, then the leader or care giver can read the question to the child.*) Some cards don't have a number because they are surprise cards with special instructions on them. Let's see if we can answer all the questions in this game."

DISCUSSION

It is often hard for children to say no to sexual abuse because they are taught to obey adults and to respect authority figures. A vital step in the process of teaching personal safety skills is to help children understand when it is appropriate to assert themselves in potentially dangerous situations. This activity can be helpful in reinforcing for children the concept of saying "No" when they are faced with a situation that is abusive. However, the therapist should use caution when employing this activity so that children are not left with feelings of guilt for not having said "No" during the abuse.

GAME BOARD

THE OKAY TO SAY NO GAME

-15-
Mom tells you to brush your teeth before you go to bed.

-14-
Dad tells you not to cross the street until the light turns green.

-10-
A man stops his car and asks you for directions.

-13-
A nice lady comes to your house and asks if she can use your phone.

-11-
Your babysitter says you can stay up later if you let her touch your privates.

-12-
Mom tells you to feed the dog.

-9-
Mom tells you it's time to take your medicine.

-8-
Your doctor tells you he has to check your privates.

-7-
Dad tells you to stop picking on your sister.

-6-
Your uncle tells you to touch his penis.

-5-
Your friend asks you to steal a chocolate bar.

-1-
Mom asks you to clean your room.

-2-
A stranger asks you to come see his puppy.

-3-
Dad tells you to put a coat on before you go outside to play.

-4-
Your babysitter tells you it's time to go to bed.

Preschool—Latency
Red Light/Green Light

MODALITY: Group

GOAL: To help children be able to differentiate between safe and unsafe touching and to teach personal safety skills.

MATERIALS

➤ Red and green construction paper or poster board or cellophane

➤ Masking tape

➤ Situation Cards: "Red Light, Green Light" *following*

METHOD

ADVANCE PREPARATION:
Using the construction paper, the group leader constructs a red "stop" light, and a green "go" light (one set per child). Another option is to use red and green cellophane for the children to look through.

ACTIVITY:

The group begins by playing the game "Red Light, Green Light." To play this game, the group leader makes two parallel lines a good distance apart. (Masking tape can be used to make the lines.) One child is chosen to be the police officer and he stands in front of one line. The other children stand behind the opposite line.

The police officer turns his back to the other children and calls out "green light!" Then he counts to three while the other children walk quickly toward him. Once the police officer has counted to three, he yells "red light!" and the players must freeze instantly. The police officer turns around to catch any players who are moving. Anyone who moves has to return to the starting line. The game continues until a player crosses the finish line.

Following this game, each child is provided with a red light and a green light made out of the colored paper. The group leader states that she is going to read out situations. For each situation, the children must decide if it is safe or unsafe. If it is a safe situation, then the children hold up their green "go" lights. If the situation is unsafe, then the children hold up their red "stop" lights. (Certain situations are deliberately ambiguous to stimulate discussion). At the end of the game the group leader can state: "If somebody goes through a red stop light, someone can get hurt. Laws are made to keep people safe. If somebody goes through a red stop light, that person has broken the law. If someone uses a secret or bad touch with a child, that person has broken the law and the child should report that crime to an adult."

DISCUSSION

Further victimization is prevented by teaching children about situations that can be potentially abusive or exploitive. The activity also reinforces the concept that sexual abuse is a crime that must be reported. Note that this activity should be done with children who have already learned the concepts of "good," "bad," and "secret" touch. (See *A Very Touching Book* by Jan Hindman.)

404

RED LIGHT, GREEN LIGHT SITUATIONS

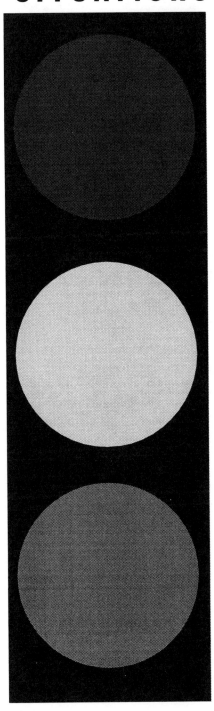

Your mom gives you a big kiss before you go to bed.

Your baby-sitter shows you his penis.

Your brother takes some money from your father's wallet without asking permission.

Your grandfather gives you a piggy back ride.

Your neighbor invites you in to see newborn puppies.

Your older sister asks you to touch her vagina and tells you not to tell mom.

Your doctor touches your private parts during a checkup.

Your cousin tells you he will give you a chocolate bar if you let him take naked pictures of you.

Your friend dares you to take a piece of gum from the store when the owner is not looking.

Your aunt asks you for a kiss after she gives you a birthday present.

Preteen—Teen
The Dating Game

MODALITY: Group

GOAL: To prevent further victimization, by teaching adolescent girls about situations that may be potentially abusive

MATERIALS

➤ Magazines with pictures of adolescent males

➤ "Bachelor Descriptions *following*

➤ Questions & Bachelor Responses *following*

➤ 4 envelopes

➤ 3 chairs

➤ Index cards (one per group member)

METHOD

ADVANCE PREPARATION:
The group leader selects pictures of adolescent males from magazines to represent the "bachelors" in the "dating game." The pictures are cut out and each one is glued onto a separate piece of paper. The "Bachelor Descriptions" are cut out and each one is glued under a

different picture. The pictures with the bachelor descriptions are each taped onto a different chair. The "Bachelor Questions" are written on the front of the envelopes (one question per envelope) and the "Bachelor Responses" to each question are placed inside the envelope which is then sealed.

ACTIVITY:

The group members sit facing the three chairs with the "bachelors" on them. Each bachelor description is read aloud to the group. Group members are selected to read the questions, open the envelopes and read the bachelor responses aloud to the group. (As an alternative, group members can develop their own bachelor descriptions and make up questions and answers.)

Group members are then provided with index cards to write which bachelor they would choose for themselves and why. Group members take turns reading their responses. The group leader encourages discussion of the responses. For a closing activity, the group members can each write their own descriptions of "The ideal Bachelor." Another closing activity is for the group members to write a "Dating Bill of Rights" that would include statements such as, "I have the right to be respected"; I have the right to say no"; I have the right to express my feelings", etc.

DISCUSSION

Many sexual abuse victims will seek out relationships that are abusive, because they have internalized the idea that they are "unworthy." Moreover, many teens lack appropriate judgment in their choice of relationships because they have been exposed to poor role models. Psychoeducational activities that focus on teaching young women the danger signs of abusive relationships, coupled with exercises that enhance self-esteem are important in order to help prevent further victimization. The "dating game" is likely to elicit a

PAPER DOLLS AND PAPER AIRPLANES

great deal of discussion among the group members. The leader should be cautious not to impose his/her own values onto the clients. If some group members are portraying poor judgment in their choice of bachelors, then the leader can encourage the group members to challenge the choices.

Questions for further group discussion include:

- Do sexual abuse victims often choose mates who treat them poorly? If so, why?

- What are some danger signs that tell you a relationship is abusive?

- What kind of a relationship do/did your parents have and how has this affected whom you might choose for yourself?

- What qualities do you think are important in a relationship?

BACHELOR DESCRIPTIONS

BACHELOR #1

Steve is the captain of the school football team. He is very popular, has a good sense of humor, and the girls describe him as a "hunk." He says he is looking for a girl who is "sexy and likes to party." He knows he can get what he wants in a relationship, because he is a "smooth talker." He admits that he has a bad temper, but he says he would never hit a girl—unless she "asked for it."

BACHELOR #2

Brandon describes himself as average—looking. He doesn't care about fashion or about making a lot of money. He likes to be romantic and make a girl feel "special." He is looking for someone who is kind, intelligent, and honest.

BACHELOR #3

Shawn is 22-years-old, but he likes to date younger girls. He says he hangs out at school dances in the hopes of finding a girl who is "cute" and will treat him with "respect." He says one thing he won't put up with in a relationship is a girl who is a "flirt." Shawn has a well-paying job, and he is looking for a girl to take for a ride in his new red Porsche.

QUESTIONS & BACHELOR RESPONSES

QUESTION #1
What would you do if we were kissing and you got really turned on and I told you I wasn't ready to go any further?

Bachelor #1:
I'd tell you I could get it with any other girl and to stop being such a prude.

Bachelor #2:
I guess I'd accept it, but I'd be frustrated and disappointed.

Bachelor #3:
When girls say "no"—they really mean "yes."

QUESTION #2
What would you do if we were going out and you didn't like what I was wearing?

Bachelor #1:
I'd ask you to put on something that makes you look better, because I wouldn't want to be embarrassed being seen with you like that.

Bachelor #2:
I don't really care what people wear.

Bachelor #3:
I'd tell you if you want to go out, you'll have to change into something nice.

QUESTION #3
What would you do if we were going out and my best friend, who was very attractive, made a pass at you?

Bachelor #1:
I'd go for it, because life's too short to miss any opportunities!

Bachelor #2:
I'd tell her I was dating you, and I'm not interested.

Bachelor #3:
I'd go for it because no girl friend is going to tell me what I can and cannot do!

QUESTION #4:
What would you do if a male friend told you he had been sexually abused?

Bachelor #1:
I'd think he was a fag, so I'd stop hanging around with him.

Bachelor #2:
I'd tell him I was willing to listen if he wanted to talk about it.

Bachelor #3:
I'd tell him I would beat up the person who abused him.

Preteen—Teen
Sticky Situations

MODALITY: Group

GOAL: To help prevent further sexual victimization by teaching teens about situations that may be potentially abusive or exploitive and to enhance problem-solving skills

MATERIALS

➤ "Sticky Situation" Cards *following*

➤ Blank "Sticky Situations" Cards (one per group member)

➤ Cardboard or poster board

➤ Scissors

➤ Pens

METHOD

ADVANCE PREPARATION:
The "Sticky Situations" cards are cut out and each one is mounted onto a piece of cardboard or poster board.

ACTIVITY:
The "Sticky Situations" cards are randomly distributed among the group members. Group members are provided with time to complete their cards by reading the situation, ranking the decision, explaining

the reason for the ranking, and describing how they would have handled the situation. Each group member then shares cards and answers with the group. The leader encourages discussion about the situations and the group is provided with an opportunity to challenge and debate peer responses. Group members can then create their own "Sticky Situations" by using the blank cards.

DISCUSSION

Many children who have been sexually abused are vulnerable to becoming re-victimized. Therapeutic interventions must not only be focused on the child's previous abuse experiences, but also on preventing further victimization and exploitation. This activity enables teens to enhance problem-solving and assertiveness skills that will help to equip them to deal with unsafe situations.

STICKY SITUATION

Jill sees an advertisement in the newspaper that says if she sends in $50.00 and a photograph of herself, she might be chosen to star in a television show. She is very excited because she has always wanted to be on TV, and she decides to send in the money and picture.

DECISION

Good   Fair   Poor

REASON

_____

What I would do

_____

STICKY SITUATION

Brenda is on a date with a popular guy on the football team. He wants to have sexual intercourse with her, but she does not feel ready. She decides to go along with what he wants, because she is worried that if she doesn't, he won't like her, and he'll spread bad rumors about her at school.

DECISION

Good   Fair   Poor

REASON

_____

What I would do

_____

STICKY SITUATION

Margaret had a friend named Kisha. They told each other everything. Kisha confided to Margaret that her stepfather was showing her pornographic movies and telling her it was to teach her about sex. It made her feel really weird. He made her promise to keep it a secret. Margaret decided she would tell her teacher—even though it meant breaking a promise.

DECISION

Good   Fair   Poor

REASON

_____

What I would do

_____

STICKY SITUATION

Bryan was being sexually abused by a guy who was a good friend of his family. This guy was lots of fun and took Bryan to baseball games. Bryan really liked lots of things they did together. Bryan was afraid if he told about the abuse, he wouldn't get to see his friend anymore and other people might think he was gay. He decided not to tell he was being sexually abused.

DECISION

Good   Fair   Poor

REASON

_____

What I would do

_____

STICKY SITUATION

Tamara got into a big fight with her boyfriend. He became very angry and hit her. He told Tamara that it was her fault, because she made him so upset. After he hit her, Tamara told her boyfriend that she did not want to see him anymore. But when her boyfriend apologized and promised he would never hit her again, Tamara decided to give him another chance.

DECISION
Good   Fair   Poor

REASON

_____

What I would do

_____

STICKY SITUATION

Laura felt she had made a big mistake. Ever since she told that her older brother had sexually abused her, her life was coming apart. Her brother had to go live with her grandparents and her mom was crying all the time. Laura felt that everything was her fault. Laura decided to say that she had made the whole thing up.

DECISION
Good   Fair   Poor

REASON

_____

What I would do

_____

STICKY SITUATION

After baseball practice, Shawn's coach invited him over for pizza. The coach put on a video of adults having sex with children. The coach tells Shawn that if he agrees to allow the coach to film him naked, he will make Shawn the captain of the baseball team. Shawn refuses and leaves. When he gets home, he does not tell anyone about what happened.

DECISION

Good   Fair   Poor

REASON

_____

What I would do

_____

STICKY SITUATION

Ariel's teacher gives her a detention because she cheated on a test. He tells her that unless she touches his penis, he will call her parents and inform them that she cheated. She decides to go along with the teacher. Afterwards, she tells her best friend about what happened, but she makes her promise not to tell anyone.

DECISION

Good   Fair   Poor

REASON

_____

What I would do

_____

STICKY SITUATION

Carrie is at a party where all her friends are drinking beer. Carrie really hates the taste of beer, but she decides to drink it because she is worried that her friends will think she is a loser if she doesn't. One of her friends (who also had been drinking) offers her a ride home. She decides to accept the ride because she is scared that if she calls her parents for a ride, they will find out she was drinking.

DECISION
Good   Fair   Poor

REASON

_____

What I would do

_____

STICKY SITUATION

Sasha goes to the doctor because she has a sore throat. The doctor explains that he needs to examine her whole body in order to find out what is wrong with her. The doctor rubs her breasts and her vagina. This makes Sasha feel very uncomfortable, but she is too shy to say anything. Afterwards, her mother sees that she is upset, but Sasha says that everything is fine, because she is too embarrassed to talk about it.

DECISION
Good   Fair   Poor

REASON

_____

What I would do

_____

Preteen—Teen
Graffiti

MODALITY: Individual, group

GOAL: To reinforce concepts of personal safety, and to enable children to express and resolve feelings associated with sexual abuse

MATERIALS

➤ Banner Paper

➤ Slogans: "Personal Safety" *following*

➤ Wallpaper remnants with a brick pattern, or mural paper

➤ Jumbo-size markers, paint, or spray paint

➤ Large plastic drop cloth

➤ Worksheet: "Graffiti Wall" *following*

METHOD

ADVANCE PREPARATION:
Tape a large plastic drop cloth under the banner paper to protect the walls and floors. Tape the banner paper to the wall.

ACTIVITY:

The activity begins by having each group member spray paint his/her name on the mural paper. This leads into a discussion about graffiti (where kids have seen it, how it is used as a form of communication, etc). The purpose of the activity is to create a non-threatening way to express feelings about sexual abuse and to highlight messages of personal safety.

Each group member is provided with a handout of "Personal Safety" slogans. Group members select slogans from the handout (or write their own) and design logos or symbols for the slogans. The slogans and logos are painted onto the "brick" wallpaper. The group can then admire their efforts. Smaller versions of the graffiti can be copied onto the individual "Graffiti Wall" worksheets.

DISCUSSION

This activity reinforces concepts of personal safety using a fun and creative medium. The activity can be used on its own or added at the end of a session on personal safety. If used in a group setting, the activity encourages group cohesiveness.

HANDOUT

SLOGANS: PERSONAL SAFETY

Sexual Abuse Is a Crime!

It's OK to Say No to Sexual Abuse!

My Body Belongs to Me!

No Means No!

Stop Crimes Against Children!

Everyone Has the Right to Be Safe And Free!

Safe Sex or No Sex!

There Is No Love in Sexual Abuse!

Handle With Care!

Kids Have Rights!

I Have a Right to Be Treated With Respect!

WORKSHEET

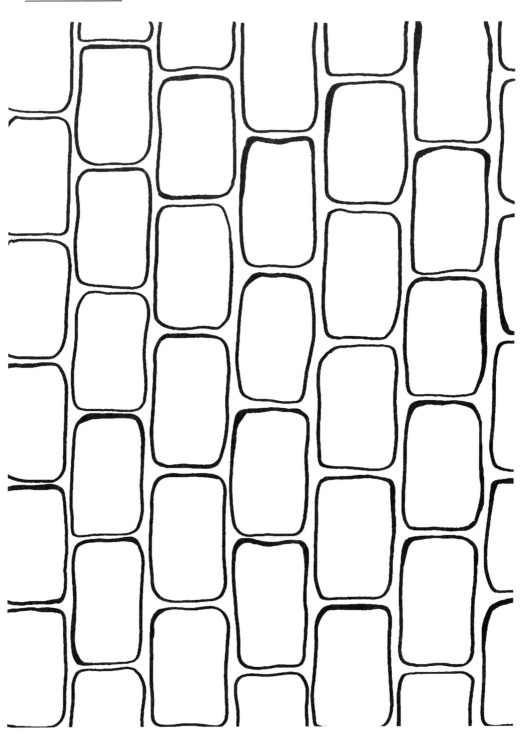

GRAFFITI

Children express their feelings as they spray paint sexual abuse slogans. This exercise is both cathartic and empowering.

Preschool—Teen
Kidzspace

MODALITY: Individual, group

GOAL: To affirm children's boundaries; to build positive self-esteem

MATERIALS

➤ Large sheets cut from a roll of mural paper

➤ Masking tape

➤ Scissors

➤ Markers

➤ Magazines

➤ Glue

➤ Signs and Symbols *following*

➤ Construction paper and mural paper

METHOD

ADVANCE PREPARATION:
Make sure children have a large enough area to do this activity.
Collect all the materials and have them ready for the activity.

ACTIVITY:

Tell group members that the activity consists of creating a special "place of their own." From a large roll of mural paper, have children select a length of paper of their choosing. Each member then finds a place and tapes his/her paper to the floor.

The leader then shows group members what materials are available. The therapist tells the children they are free to use the materials in any way they choose. They can use the signs and symbols provided (or design their own signs and symbols); they can cut the paper any size or shape; build walls, construct shelters, buildings; make a list of who is and who is not allowed in their space, etc.

The therapist offers a few simple rules:

1. Everyone has 20 minutes.

2. While you're creating your space, we will work in silence.

3. At the end of the construction period, we will have a group tour and visit each child's space.

Once completed, children can take group members on a "guided tour" of their Kidzspace "kreations."

DISCUSSION

This activity is often enhanced by playing music. Depending on the needs of the group, the leader could select energizing or relaxing music. It helps to create a sense of safety as well. Children are encouraged to decorate and design their space by using scraps of paper, fabric, and various other objects.

Through this activity, children begin to learn they have rights and responsibilities. The therapist creates an opportunity for each member to have an experience to plan and create a safety zone. For children whose bodies and spirits have been violated, this is extremely important. It can form the beginning steps in children learning to define their boundaries.

SIGNS & SYMBOLS

KEEP
A SAFE
DISTANCE

I CAN TOUCH
MY PRIVATES,
IN PRIVATE

ASK
BEFORE
YOU ENTER

PETS ALLOWED!

FRAGILE!

PETS

Chapter 13
Self-Esteem

PURPOSE OF THE CHAPTER:

Self-esteem building is a life-long process. A child's perception of self is fed by many diverse experiences beginning with neonatal care and continuing in the experience of being parented and cared for.

This chapter looks specifically at self-esteem issues as they may relate to the sexual abuse. Each activity is aimed at providing the child with a forum through which to regain an aspect of self-esteem that may have been affected by the sexual abuse.

The context is forward looking; that is, assisting the child in setting his/her sights on regaining a positive sense of self. This will enable the child to move on — to be able to "ground" the sexual abuse experience, assigning the experience to a place in his or her emotional development which can be integrated. The activities are also designed to give the child opportunities to separate who they are from what happens to them.

Given the ongoing process of self-esteem building, it is essential to also provide care givers with ways to understand and enhance the child's strengths. Messages and communications from care givers on a daily basis are more powerful than what can be provided in any treatment intervention. These activities are, therefore, greatly enhanced by working in conjunction with care givers in meeting these therapeutic goals.

Preschool
Superstar

MODALITY: Group

GOALS: To affirm the strength and courage exhibited by victims who disclose sexual abuse; to instill a belief in a positive future

MATERIALS

- ➤ Cardboard
- ➤ "Star" patterns *following*
- ➤ Glitter
- ➤ Glue
- ➤ Scissors
- ➤ Sparklers (available at party supply stores)
- ➤ Paints or markers

METHOD

ADVANCE PREPARATION:
Pre-cut the star shapes on cardboard for each child. Group members then decorate the stars with paint and glitter.

ACTIVITY:
The next part of this activity consists of awarding the stars. This can be done in a number of ways. Group members can award themselves a star, making a positive statement, such as, "I'm awarding myself this

star because I was afraid my mom would get mad, and I still was brave enough to tell." Group members can award each other stars and make positive statements. A powerful way of awarding stars is to have care givers award the stars to their children and to make positive statements.

The last part of the activity consists of teaching the children and care givers this song (sung to "Twinkle, Twinkle Little Star" melody):

> *"Twinkle Twinkle Superstar*
> *How I wonder what you are*
> *I can hardly wait to see*
> *When you grow up what you'll be*
> *Twinkle Twinkle Superstar*
> *How I wonder what you are."*

The tune is familiar to almost all children and their care givers. When everyone knows the words, the therapist hands out sparklers to the care givers. Each care giver explains to his/her child how to handle the sparkler and then ignites the sparkler. The group then sings "Twinkle Twinkle Superstar" until the sparklers extinguish.

DISCUSSION

This activity is an important opportunity to assist parents in acquiring skills to support their children. A useful step is to meet with parents prior to using this activity. The therapist can explain the goals and objectives of the exercise. Parents can be encouraged to give verbal and non-verbal messages about the preciousness of each child.

There is a special festive air to the closing activity. This affirms each child's worth and celebrates the bond between care givers and child.

STAR PATTERNS

436

Preschool—Latency
The Lollipop Tree

MODALITY: Group

GOAL: To enhance self-esteem

MATERIALS

➤ Worksheet: "Lollipop Tree" *following*

➤ Crayons (red, green, yellow, orange, purple)

➤ White tagboard or poster board

➤ Popsicle sticks or tongue depressors

➤ Lollipops hung on a lollipop tree

METHOD

ADVANCE PREPARATION:
Make five different colored lollipops (red, green, yellow, orange, purple) by cutting out white tagboard circles, coloring each one a different color, and taping each one onto a popsicle stick or tongue depressor. Write one question on each cardboard lollipop:

- Everyone in this group is special. What is special about you?

- Everyone in this group is brave. Tell about a brave thing that you did.

- Everyone in this group should feel proud. What do you feel proud about?

- Everyone in this group can try their hardest. What do you try hard at?

- Everyone in this group can have a happy future. What do you want to be when you grow up?

The lollipop tree should also be prepared before the group session. There are various ways to make a lollipop tree: Green poster board or foam board covered with green wrapping paper can be cut into the shape of a tree or the candy lollipops can be taped onto a tree-shaped plant.

ACTIVITY:
Each child is provided with a "Lollipop Tree" worksheet and a set of crayons. The leader explains: "I have some important questions to ask the group. Once a question has been answered, you can color in a lollipop on your tree. Once all the lollipops have been colored in, I have a surprise to share with the group."

The leader begins by reading aloud the first question from the red tagboard lollipop ("Everyone in this group is special. What is special about you?"). One child is chosen to answer the question and then the other children can add their responses. Once the question has been answered, the children color in one of the lollipops on their worksheet red. The activity continues until the five questions have been answered and the five lollipops on the worksheet have been colored in. The leader then reveals the lollipop tree to the children, and each child can pick a lollipop off the tree.

CLOSING ACTIVITY:

The group stands in a circle. The therapist leads the children in the following exercise:

- If you know someone who thinks you're special, clap your hands!

- If you know someone who thinks you're brave, thump your chest!

- If you know someone who says the secret touching is not your fault, stand up tall!

- If you know someone who sees you do your best, touch the sky!

- If you know someone who loves you, touch your heart!

DISCUSSION

Young children will be enchanted with the concept of a lollipop tree. The activity is certain to capture the children's interest and help them strengthen their self-esteem. The closing exercise reinforces the ideas from the activity.

LOLLIPOP TREE WORKSHEET

Latency—Teen

The Feeling Good Every Day Game

MODALITY: Group

GOAL: To enhance self-esteem and to encourage children to incorporate self-care into their daily lives

MATERIALS

- ➤ 2 pieces of poster board
- ➤ Game Board: "Feeling Good Every Day" *following*
- ➤ Markers
- ➤ Happy face stickers (one per child)
- ➤ Star stickers (one per child)
- ➤ Hershey's Kisses (one per child)

METHOD

ADVANCE PREPARATION:

The therapist copies the "Feeling Good Every Day Game" onto a large piece of poster board. The second piece of poster board is used for the game cards and is cut into 35 squares, approximately 2"x3". The cards are numbered from 1 to 31 (write the number large in the center of the card). The remaining four cards are used for "surprise" game cards. Write one of the following statements on each of the surprise cards: "You have a nice smile! Take a happy face sticker and give one to each player who shows you her nice smile"; "You are special! Take a Hershey's Kiss and give one to each player"; "Ask someone in the group for a hug"; "You are a superstar. Take a star sticker and give one to each player." The game cards are arranged so they are not in order, and the "surprise" cards are interspersed among the deck of game cards.

ACTIVITIES:

Players sit in a circle with the game board in the middle and the game cards placed face down beside the game board. The group leader begins by asking the children what *self-esteem* means. If nobody in the group can give a definition, then the leader can state: "*Self-esteem* means how you feel about yourself. If you like yourself, you have high self-esteem. If you feel bad about yourself, you have low self-esteem. We are going to play a game about self-esteem that will help us to think about ways we can feel better about ourselves."

The game is described as follows: "Players take turns picking the game card at the top of the pile of cards. The number on the card corresponds with a question on the game board for the player to read aloud and answer. There are four surprise cards in the deck. The game is finished once all the cards have been used. In this game, there are no losers—only winners!"

DISCUSSION

Many children, particularly those who have been sexually victimized, have very poor self-esteem. Although this activity is not going to repair a child's damaged self-concept, it can be used as a beginning point to enable children to feel better about themselves.

GAME BOARD

THE FEELING GOOD
EVERY DAY GAME

Monday	Tuesday	Wednesday	Thursday	Friday	Saturday	Sunday
1 Define self-esteem.	2 Name 3 things that you like about yourself.	3 Fill in the blank: "I'm proud of myself when..."	4 Say something nice to the person on your left	5 What is one thing that really cheers you up?	6 Tell about something you have done well this week.	7 What are 2 things you can do to feel better when you are upset?
8 Tell about something nice you once did for someone.	9 What is one thing you really enjoy doing at school?	10 What is the one thing you like best about yourself?	11 Fill in the blank: "I feel smart because..."	12 What is the bravest thing you have ever done?	13 True or false: There is no such thing as a perfect person.	14 Fill in the blank: "one thing I do better than most people is _____."
15 What is one thing you really enjoy doing at home?	16 What is something you need when you are upset?	17 Tell about the happiest moment of your life	18 Who is someone you can talk to when you are upset?	19 Name 3 things that are special about you.	20 Fill in the blank: "Something about myself I can change is _____."	21 Tell about something that makes you feel good.
22 What is something you can tell yourself when you are upset?	23 Say something nice to the person on your right.	24 Name 3 things that make you laugh.	25 What would a friend say she likes best about you?	26 What is something you really enjoy doing?	27 Tell about something nice someone did for you.	28 Fill in the blank: "Next time I am upset I will..."
29 What is something you can do when someone hurts you?	30 Fill in the blank: "I feel special when..."	31 What is something you are looking forward to?				

Preteen—Latency
Fortune Teller

MODALITY: Individual, group

GOALS: To instill a positive outlook for the future; to reinforce concept that children are never to blame for sexual abuse

MATERIALS

➤ Blank paper

➤ Stickers (animals and simple shapes are best for the activity)

➤ Worksheet: "Fortune Teller" *following*

➤ Scissors

➤ Pens

METHOD

ADVANCE PREPARATION:
The therapist should copy the "Fortune Teller" worksheets to give to group members.

ACTIVITY:
The leader distributes the worksheets to group members and

demonstrates how to cut and fold them into fortune tellers. Each group member decorates a fortune teller. The group can then play with their fortune tellers.

A second part to this activity can be added, if desired. It involves having the children make up their own positive messages and write them on other fortune tellers they construct. In preparation for this step, the therapist may need to brainstorm a list of possible messages kids need to hear.

DISCUSSION

Folded-paper (see fortune tellers have captivated children through the ages. When this activity is combined with positive messages about the innocence of childhood (how children can never be responsible for sexual abuse), the effect can be powerful. The activity can be expanded to take a full session or it can be used as an effective warm-up or closing activity in almost any theme.

FORTUNE TELLER

Your body belongs to you!

Trust Your Feelings!

Some secrets are NOT okay to keep!

Sexual abuse is never a kid's fault!

mistakes make sometimes Adults

Hugs are great if you want them

You have a right to say no!

You have a right to be safe!

- -

Cut along dotted line

1. With plain side up, fold paper in half, open, then fold in half in the other direction.

2. Fold corners into center.

3. Turn sheet over and again fold corners into center.

4. Fold in half; open, then fold in half in the other direction.

5. Insert thumb and index fingers inside numbered corners. Press corners (A) into center to open.

6. Have someone pick a number (i.e. 4). Open and close in alternating directions 4 times. With triangles exposed, have person choose a number or symbol. Open and close as you spell the word (i.e. horse = 5 times). Now have them select another color or symbol. Lift triangle and read corresponding message.

Latency—Teen
Self-Esteem Questionnaire

MODALITY: Individual, group

GOAL: To assess child's level of self-esteem and to promote awareness related to self-image

MATERIALS

➤ Questionnaire: "Self-Esteem" *following*

➤ Pencils

METHOD

ADVANCE PREPARATION:
The group leader makes copies of the questionnaire for group members.

ACTIVITY:
Each child completes the questionnaire. The responses are then shared with the group.

DISCUSSION

Children who have been sexually abused often think poorly of themselves because of the negative messages they have been given. This questionnaire is aimed at assessing the specific factors that contribute to a child's negative self-concept. This assessment activity can be used to precede one of the treatment activities in this chapter.

SELF-ESTEEM QUESTIONNAIRE

Self-esteem means how you feel about yourself. If you have high self-esteem, that means you like yourself. If you have low self-esteem, that means you feel bad about yourself. Rate the following statement to show how you feel about yourself.

QUESTION

Statement	Always	Sometimes	Never
I like myself.	☐	☐	☐
I think other people like me.	☐	☐	☐
I feel I can't do anything right.	☐	☐	☐
I can make friends.	☐	☐	☐
I feel I am bad because I let the abuse happen.	☐	☐	☐
I feel people think I'm weird because I was sexually abused.	☐	☐	☐
I feel dirty because I was touched in a sexual way.	☐	☐	☐
I feel good because I told about the sexual abuse.	☐	☐	☐
I do well in school.	☐	☐	☐
I feel loved by my family.	☐	☐	☐
I like the way I look.	☐	☐	☐
I think I have good ideas.	☐	☐	☐
I get into trouble.			

	Always	Sometimes	Never
I feel left out of things.	☐	☐	☐
I am a kind person.	☐	☐	☐
I feel brave.	☐	☐	☐
I get into fights.	☐	☐	☐
I feel happy to be me.	☐	☐	☐
I believe I have a bright future.	☐	☐	☐
	☐	☐	☐

For Younger Children

Latency—Teen
Bravo Bingo

MODALITY: Group

GOAL: To enhance self-esteem and to affirm bravery of disclosure

FOR OLDER CHILDREN:

MATERIALS

➤ Blank "Bravo Cards" *following*

➤ Sheet of "Bravo Statements" *following*

➤ Bingo markers or counters

➤ Glue

➤ Scissors

➤ Prizes (star stickers)

➤ Decorated gift boxes or gift bags

METHOD

ADVANCE PREPARATION:

The group leader makes copies of the "Bravo Card" for each group member. In addition, make copies of the "Bravo Statements: For Older Children" so that each child has one. Make an extra copy of this statement sheet to cut into sections. To make the prize, place the star stickers (enough for each group member) in decorative gift box.

On the inside of the box, write the following message: "You can reach for the stars and create your own future!" Take a star sticker and give on to each group member.

ACTIVITY:

Each child chooses 24 of the 35 statements and glues them, in any order, on a "Bravo Card." While group members are constructing their cards, cut up another statement sheet and fold each statement so it can't be seen. Place these statements in a bag for the bingo caller.

Group members play bingo as usual. When a player wins by getting a straight or diagonal line, he or she calls out, "Bravo!" The winner opens the gift box, reads the messgae aloud to the group, and distributes the star stickers.

FOR YOUNGER CHILDREN:

MATERIALS

- ➤ "Hero Card" (1 for each player) *following*
- ➤ "Hero Statements" (1 for each player) *following*
- ➤ Scissors
- ➤ Glue
- ➤ Prizes

METHOD

ADVANCE PREPARATION:

The group leader should copy and cut out the "hero" star cards so that each child will have four stars. In addition, make copies of the statements so that there are plenty for the children to choose.

ACTIVITY:

A variation of this game can be played with younger children. Children are to choose four of their favorite statements from the list of ten and glue them onto their star "hero" cards.

DISCUSSION

This activity gives group members an opportunity to choose positive statements about themselves. There is considerable repetition and members can exercise some choice as there are 35 statements and only 24 are needed to design a Bravo Card.

The star stickers and accompanying message "You can reach for the stars and create your own future" gives children a sense of hope about their future. This is a crucial step in the trauma recovery process.

BRAVO CARD

B	R	A	V	O
		FREE		

BRAVO STATEMENTS: FOR OLDER CHILDREN

I can ask for a hug if I want one.	I am lovable and valuable!	It's OK to be upset when you talk about sexual abuse.	I am a kind and caring person.	I know how to play fair.	I am a good listener.	People listen to me when I talk about what happened.
When people say mean things to me, I can say stop!	There is nobody else just like me!	I can do my best.	I can create my own future.	I know some secrets are not OK to keep.	I know I have a right to be safe.	I am a good friend.
I can think nice thoughts.	I can be a good friend to myself.	I can make good decisions.	My body is precious.	I am learning to take care of myself.	I'm sharing my feelings with my friends in group.	People believe I was brave to tell.
I know nobody is perfect.	I am happy to be me!	I have a right to say "yes" to good touching.	All my feelings are OK.	I have a right to say "no" to secret touch.	I can talk to a trusted adult if I'm feeling upset.	I feel I did the right thing by telling about the sexual abuse.
Kids who tell about sexual abuse are brave!	I can let out my hurt by talking to someone.	I can think of safe ways to express my feelings.	It takes courage to deal with sexual abuse.	I know it's OK to cry when I'm upset.	The more I talk about what happened, the easier it gets.	I believe talking about my feelings will help me feel better.

HERO CARDS: FOR YOUNGER CHILDREN

HERO

BRAVO STATEMENTS: FOR YOUNGER CHILDREN

I AM
BRAVE!

I AM
LOVEABLE!

MY FEELINGS
ARE OK!

I CAN
ASK FOR
A HUG!

I CAN TALK TO
AN ADULT IF
I'M FEELING
SAD

SOME
SECRETS ARE
NOT OK!

IT'S OK TO SAY
NO!

I CAN
SHARE WITH
MY FRIENDS

I AM A SUPER
KID!

KIDS WHO
TELL ABOUT
SECRET
TOUCH ARE
HEROES!

Latency—Teen

Protest March

MODALITY: Group

GOALS: To enhance self esteem; to understand the impact of societal attitudes on sexual abuse victims

MATERIALS

- ➤ Popsicle sticks
- ➤ Blank index cards
- ➤ Scissors
- ➤ Glue
- ➤ Markers
- ➤ Magazines
- ➤ List: "Possible Slogans" *following*

METHOD

ADVANCE PREPARATION:
Glue popsicle sticks to 5"x5" blank cards to resemble miniature protest signs. It is a good idea to have one already made as a model.

ACTIVITY:
This activity begins with a discussion of what you can do when you're upset about something. If there is a newspaper or magazine account of a protest march, this is an excellent way to introduce the concept of protests.

Have group members brainstorm different slogans and record them on a chalkboard or flip chart paper. The next part of the activity involves each group member constructing a placard and sharing it with the group.

DISCUSSION

This activity is a good way to discuss society's attitudes toward sexual abuse. Older children and adolescents may benefit from writing a letter to a newspaper, magazine, or to a member of government. Activities of this nature are empowering and affirming.

The slogans can also be used with "Myths and Facts" in Chapter 1.

PAPER DOLLS AND PAPER AIRPLANES

POSSIBLE SLOGANS FOR PROTEST MARCH

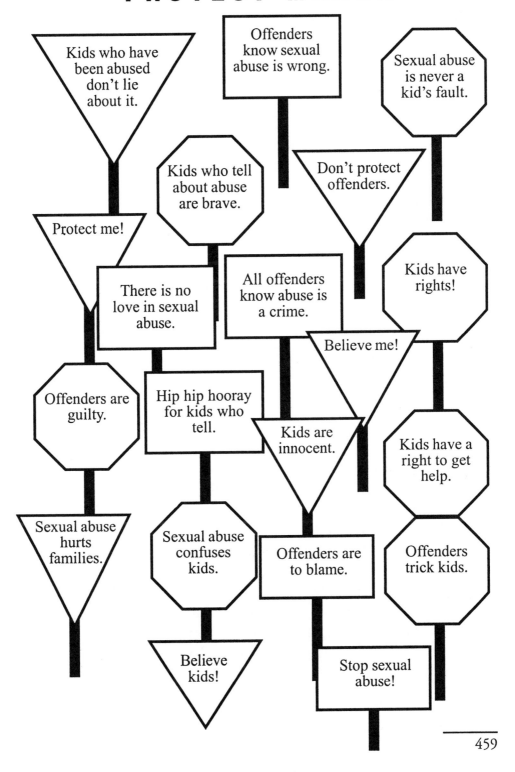

Kids who have been abused don't lie about it.

Offenders know sexual abuse is wrong.

Sexual abuse is never a kid's fault.

Kids who tell about abuse are brave.

Don't protect offenders.

Protect me!

There is no love in sexual abuse.

All offenders know abuse is a crime.

Kids have rights!

Believe me!

Offenders are guilty.

Hip hip hooray for kids who tell.

Kids are innocent.

Kids have a right to get help.

Sexual abuse hurts families.

Sexual abuse confuses kids.

Offenders are to blame.

Offenders trick kids.

Believe kids!

Stop sexual abuse!

All Ages
Layered Gift

MODALITY: Group

GOALS: To enhance self-esteem and to provide children with
opportunities to offer positive reinforcement to peers

MATERIALS

➤ Package of Hershey Kisses

➤ Worksheet: "Messages" *following*

➤ Adhesive labels

➤ Sheets of colored tissue paper

➤ Tape

METHOD

ADVANCE PREPARATION:
Copy each of the attached messages onto a separate adhesive label.
Wrap the bag of Hershey's Kisses in a layer of tissue paper. On the
tissue paper, attach the adhesive label that states: "Open this gift and
share it with the group." Wrap the gift in another layer of tissue paper
and attach one of the messages onto the tissue paper. Continue
wrapping the gift in layers, adding a different message to the outside
of each layer. Wrap the gift in many layers, ensuring there are more

layers than group members. (For example, if there are eight group members, then wrap the gift in at least nine layers).

ACTIVITY:
The leader begins the activity by announcing that there is a gift for the group and explains that whoever receives the gift must read the gift tag (what is written on the adhesive label) and follow the instructions. The first message may read: "Give this to someone who is brave."

The child selects someone in the group whom she or he thinks is brave, and passes the gift onto that person. That group member opens a layer of the gift, finds the next message, and selects another group member to pass the gift onto. This continues until the gift is handed to a group member who reads the final message: "Open this gift and share it with the group!" As the gift unfolds, the intensity builds, and excitement mounts. Each group member is assured of a positive message.

DISCUSSION

This is a short but fun activity that can be used at the end of a session following one of the other activities in this chapter. It offers group members an opportunity to value and celebrate one another. The instructions can be easily adapted for use with younger or older children. It can also be used to commemorate seasonal holidays such as Valentine's Day (a bag of chocolate hearts can be wrapped in place of Hershey's Kisses).

MESSAGES: LAYERED GIFT

Give this to someone who has a nice smile.

Give this to someone who is a good listener.

Give this to someone who is understanding.

Give this to someone who would make a good friend.

Give this to someone who has helped you with a problem.

Give this to someone who shares their feelings.

Give this to someone who looks happy to be here.

Give this to someone who is brave.

Give this to someone who has good ideas.

Give this to someone who cares about others.

Give this to someone who has made you laugh.

Give this to someone who follows the group rules.

Open this gift and share it with the group!

Conclusion
Transitions and Graduations

Saying good-bye is as important as saying hello. As with all aspects of the therapeutic process, the closure phase should be clearly articulated as to when and how the therapy will end. It is important for children to have a sense of what has been accomplished by them in order to successfully end their participation in therapy. Scrapbooks are one tool that allow children to have a lasting record of what they have worked on, and can contain both opening and closing letters from therapists.

Clinical messages should include the concept of "checkups" or "tune-ups." It is important to let children know that it is expected that they may need to "check in" again in the future with a helping professional. As children reach various developmental milestones, they may have different questions or concerns that may be best addressed by helpers who are also part of their support system.

Some children in therapy may be referred to other services. Understanding that each child has different needs at different times is a useful discussion topic as therapy nears the termination phase.

A "record" of the therapy experience, whether a scrapbook, a journal, or some other means, enables children to look back and better understand this period in their lives. "Grounding" the experience places another building block firmly in the child's recovery process.

Appendix A: **Theoretical Framework**

The theoretical framework for this book draws upon the following sources:
- Trauma studies (Terr, Van derKolk, Janoff-Bulman)
- Trauma assessment (Hindman)
- Theory and practice of group psychotherapy (Yalom)
- Sexual abuse treatment structure (James, Herman)

"What are we treating?" is perhaps the most important question guiding practice. For the authors, sexual abuse is an event or experience, not a condition. Effective treatment planning is dependent on an assessment of the impact of the sexual abuse and takes into account how the event is experienced and the developmental context in which the experience occurs. The authors follow the components outlined by Hindman (*Just Before Dawn*, 1989) in her Trauma Assessment Tool, which includes Symptomological, Relationship, Situational, and Developmental perspectives.

The treatment activities in this book are divided into preschool, latency, preteen, and teen groups in order to take into account the developmental differences among these age-groups. Therefore, it is assumed that any child placed in a sexual abuse treatment group has been assessed for both impact and developmental considerations.

With this in mind, it is important to consider that the impact of events experienced in early childhood may not be available for therapeutic intervention until a later stage of development. In fact, to some degree for many children, unresolved trauma issues may surface at various developmental milestones.

For example, a sexual abuse experience occurring during the preschool stage of development may surface during puberty. As the child's body begins to develop secondary sex characteristics, the child may be triggered psychologically:

- What do these changes mean?
- Am I now more of a sexual person and vulnerable to assault?
- Am I going to sexually assault others?

Obviously, these questions aren't likely to surface in such a clear way. More likely, the child's uncertainty will be evidenced in behavior change. This issue raises the importance of including parents and other care givers in the therapeutic process. Being educated about what to expect at various developmental milestones and what to do about it is an important component to include in the child's overall treatment plan.

The choice of treatment modality (post assessment) is sometimes determined by what resources are available. Groups may be the only service available in any given community or the only service available without a long waiting period. From a purely clinical point of view, group sessions are the treatment of choice for the following reasons:

- The child is able to make use of peer support.
- The dynamics of secrecy and isolation need to be addressed in a structured format.
- There is a need for a normalization process (responses and reactions to the experience).
- There is a demonstrated need to learn the skills involved in receiving and giving support.
- There is a need to provide a forum through which shameful events can be shared, witnessed, and accepted by peers.
- There is a need to observe adult role models who work with embarrassing, difficult material in a constructive and helpful manner.
- There is a need to participate in a peer process that brings closure to the process with a look toward future development.

Most children will benefit from group process at some time in their recovery period. Group is the only modality that provides a peer supported process for normalizing reactions and response to sexual abuse and provides a format which, by its very nature, addresses the issues of secrecy and isolation. The timing of this intervention depends on the treatment needs of the child at the time of referral and the availability of resources.

When group is recommended, the authors support a parent/child model. For preschool children, this means shared time at the beginning and end of group when parents and children work together in the same room at the same time. For older children, parent's groups conducted at the same time as children's groups (same location, but separate rooms) is recommended.

The content, format, and structure of the parent's group can vary according to the needs presented by the families requesting service. The issues important to consider are:

- Information on sexual abuse and its effects
- Developmental expectations
- The systems involved in responding to sexual abuse occurrence
- Content and process of material and activities utilized in the children's groups.

It is felt that parents need an opportunity to review, discuss, understand, and support the activities which involve their children. What happens in group is obviously a small part of the child's world. Therefore, it is critical to involve parents and primary care givers in the therapeutic process. For this reason, some children may need to be involved in dyadic or family work prior to group or some parents may need to be involved in individual work prior to and in conjunction with group work.

Equally important, parents need an opportunity to express their fears and concerns regarding what the sexual abuse experience means to their child's future. It is most helpful when parents can do this apart from their child, with group leaders who are focusing on the parent's needs while being aware at the same time of the child's needs.

The activities in this book are directive, specific, and structured. They are aimed at providing treatment interventions for children who have been traumatized. Utilizing play as a primary communication tool of children, the authors have provided a format through which children can ground their traumatic experiences through mastery of specific tasks.

While non-directive play therapy methods have historically been utilized to assist children in processing unresolved conflict, directive, structured play enables traumatized children to address issues of self-blame and cognitive distortion. This type of intervention provides a concrete means to ground and mark memory, externalize traumatic images and experiences, and make concrete the many "floating" images and distortions children are left with post-trauma.

The authors' clinical research and clinical experiences have made it clear that the treatment needs of traumatized children go beyond "labeling" and/or symbolic representation. Words can be forgotten or distorted—words were forbidden for most children sworn to secrecy. Words were used to threaten or coerce. Therefore, action, doing, and activity become the reality-based tools that allow for the safe expression of a child's past painful experiences.

Appendix B: **Bibliography**

Trauma studies and trauma assessment

Eth, S., Pynoos, R. (1985). Developmental Perspective on Psychic Trauma in Childhood. In C.R. Figley (Ed), *Trauma and Its Wake* (pp. 36-52). New York: Brunner/Mazel.

Kordich-Hall, D. (1993). *Assessing Child Trauma.* Toronto: The Institute for the Prevention of Child Abuse.

Hindman, J. (1989). *Just Before Dawn.* Oregon: AlexAndria Associates.

Terr, L.C. (1990). *Too Scared To Cry: Psychic Trauma In Childhood.* New York: Harper and Row.

Van Der Kolk, B. A. (1987). *Psychological Trauma.* Washington, D.C.: American Psychiatric Press.

Impact of child sexual abuse

Browne, A., and Finkelhor, D. (1987). Impact of Child Sexual Abuse: A Review of the Current Research. In: *Annual Progress in Child Psychiatry and Child Development.*

Conte, J. & Berliner, L. (1988). The Impact of Sexual Abuse On Children: Empirical Findings. In L. Walker (ed), *Handbook on Sexual Abuse of Children.* (pp. 72-93). New York: Springer.

Eth, S. and Pynoos, R. (eds.). (1985). *Post Traumatic Stress Disorder in Children.* Washington D.C.: American Psychiatric Press.

Gold, E.R. (1986). Long-Term Effects of Sexual Victimization in Childhood: An Attributional Approach. *Journal of Consulting and Clinical Psychology.* 54; 471-75.

Kendall-Tackett, K., Meyer-Williams, L., Finkelhor, D. (1993). Impact of Sexual Abuse on Children: A Review and Synthesis of Recent Empirical Studies. *Psychological Bulletin.* 113:1; 164-80.

Summit, R. (1983). The Child Sexual Abuse Accommodation Syndrome. *Child Abuse and Neglect.* 7; 177-93.

Treatment of child sexual abuse

Adams-Tucker, C. (1984). Early Treatment of Child incest Victims. *American journal of Psychotherapy.* 38:4; 505-15.

Friedrich, W. N., Beilke, R.L., and Urquiza, A.J. (1988). Behavior Problems in Young Sexually Abused Boys. *Journal of Interpersonal Violence.* 3: 21-28.

Giaretto, H. (1982). *Integrated Treatment of Child Sexual Abuse: A Treatment and Training Manual.* Palo Alto, Calif.: Human Sciences and Behavior Books.

Gil, E. (1991). *The Healing Power Of Play.* New York: The Guilford Press.

Hindman, J. (1991). *The Mourning Breaks.* Ontario, Oregon: AlexAndria Associates.

James, B. and Nasjileti, M. (1983). *Treating Sexually Abused Children and Their Families.* Palo Alto, Calif.: Consulting Psychologists Press.

James, B. (1989). *Treating Traumatized Children.* Lexington, Mass.: Lexington Books.

Jehu, D., Klassen C., and Gazan, M. (1986). Cognitive Restructuring of Distorted Beliefs, Associated With Childhood Sexual Abuse in *Social Work Practice in Sexual Problems* Haworth Press, Inc.: New York.

Jones, D.P.H. (1986). Individual Psychotherapy for the Sexually Abused Child. *International Journal of Child Abuse and Neglect.* 10: 377-85.

Lowenstein, L. (1995). The Resolution Scrapbook As an Aid in the Treatment of Traumatized Children. *Child Welfare.* 74:4: 889-904.

MacFarlane, K., and Cunningham, C. (1988). *Steps to Healthy Touching.* Mount Dora, Florida: Kidsrights.

MacFarlane, K., and Waterman, J., with Connerly, S., Damon, L.,Durfee, M., & Long, S. (1986). *Sexual Abuse of Young Children.* New York: The Guilford Press.

Porter, E. (1986). *Treating the Young Male Victim of Sexual Assault: Issues and Intervention Strategies.* Orwell, Vermont: Safer Society Press.

APPENDIXES

Rowe, W.S. and Savage, S. (1987). *Sexuality and the Developmentally Handicapped.* Queenston, Ontario: The Edwin Mellen Press.

Trepper, T, and Barrett, M. (1989). *Systemic Treatment of Incest.* New York: Brunner and Mazel.

Group psychotherapy

Celano, M. (1990). Activities and Games for Group Psychotherapy With Sexually Abused Children. *International Journal of Group Psychotherapy.* 40:4; 419-429.

Corder, B.F., Cornwall, T., and Whiteside, R. (1984). Techniques for Increasing Effectiveness of Co-Therapy Functioning in Adolescent Psychotherapy Groups. In: *International Journal of Group Psychotherapy.* 34:4, October.

Corey, G., Corey, M. S. (1977). *Groups: Process and Practice.* Monterey, Calif.: Brooks-Cole.

De Luca, R., Boyes, D., Furer, P., Grayston, A., Hiebert-Murphy, D. (1992). Group Treatment For Child Sexual Abuse. *Canadian Psychology.* 33:2;168-175.

Dimock, H.G. (1987). *Groups: Leadership and Group Development.* San Diego, Calif.: University Associates, Inc.

Gagliano, C. (1987). Group Treatment for Sexually Abused Girls. *Social Casework.* 68:2; 102-08.

Kitchur, M., and Bell, R. (1989). Group Psychotherapy With Preadolescent Sexual Abuse Victims: Literature Review and Description of an Inner-City Group. *International Journal of Group Psychotherapy.* 39:3; 285-309.

Nelki, J., and Watters, J. (1989). A Group for Sexually Abused Young Children: Unraveling The Web. *Child Abuse and Neglect.* 13; 369-77.

Northen, H. (1988). *Social Work With Groups.* New York: Columbia University Press.

Pescosolido, F., and Petrella, D. (1986). The Development, Process, and Evaluation of Group Psychotherapy With Sexually Abused Preschool Girls. *International Journal Group Psychotherapy.* 36:3; 447-69.

Rose, S., Edleson, J. (1987). *Working With Children and Adolescents in Groups.* San Francisco: Jossey-Bass Publishers.

Shulman, L. (1984). *The Skills of Helping Individuals and Groups.* Itasca, Ill.: F.E. Peacock Publishers.

Steward, M., Farquhar, L., Dicharry, D., Glick, D., Martin, P. (1986). Group Therapy: A Treatment of Choice for Young Victims of Child Abuse. *International Journal Group Psychotherapy.* 36:2; 261-77.

Sturkie, K. (1983). Structured Group Treatment for Sexually Abused Children. *Health and Social Work.* 8; 299-308.

Yalom, I. (1975). *The Theory and Practice of Group Psychotherapy.* New York: Basic Books.

RESOURCES

Adams, C., Fay, J., and Loreen-Martin, J. *No Is Not Enough: Helping Teenagers Avoid Sexual Assault.* San Luis, Obispo, Calif.: Impact Publishers.

Adams, C. & Fay, J. *No More Secrets.* San Luis Obispo, Calif.: Impact Publishers.

Baird, K. *My Body Belongs To Me.* Circle Pines, Minnesota: American Guidance Service, Inc.

Bannatyne-Cugnet, J. (1993). *Estelle and the Self-Esteem Machine.* Red Deer Alberta: Red Deer College Press.

Bennett Blackburn, L. (1991). *I Know I Made It happen.* Centering Corporation, Box 3367, Omaha, Nebraska 68103.

Blank, J. (1980). *The Playbook for Kids About Sex.* Down There Press.

Boston Women's Health Book Collective. *The New Our Bodies Ourselves.* Simon & Shuster, New York: 1984.

Chamberlain, N. *My Day at The Courthouse: A Book For A Child Who Will Be A Witness In Court.* West Linn, Oregon.

Cole, J. (1988). *Asking About Sex and Growing Up.* New York: William Morrow & Company.

Davis, N. *Once Upon A Time, Therapeutic Stories To Heal Abused Children.* Oxon Hill, Maryland.

Galt Toys. *Secret Kit* (Invisible Ink and Developer Markers). James Galt & Co. Ltd. Cheadle, Chesire, England.

Gawain, S. (1995). *Creative Visualization.* San Rafael, Calif.: New World Library.

Hague, K. (1989). *Bear Hugs.* New York: Henry Holt & Company.

Hartelius, M. (1991). *Zoom! The Complete Paper Airplane Kit.* New York: Grosset & Dunlop, Inc.

Hazen, B. (1987). *The Knight Who Was Afraid of the Dark.* New York: Dial Press.

Hazen, B. (1992). *Even If I Did Something Awful.* Toronto: Maxwell MacMillan, Canada.

Herzfeld, G., and Powell, R. (1986). *Coping For Kids.* West Nyack, NY: The Center for applied Research in Education.

Hindman, J. *A Very Touching Book.* Ontario Oregon: AlexAndria Associates.

Huff, Vivian. (1978). *Let's Make Paper Dolls.* New York: Harper & Row, Publishers, Inc.

Loomans, D. *The Lovables in the Kingdom of Self-Esteem.* Tiburon, Calif.: H.J. Kramer, Inc.

Marks, B. and R. (1977). *Give a Magic Show.* New York: William Morrow & Co., Inc.

Mayle, P. *Where Did I Come From?* New York: Carol Publishing Group.

Mayle, P. *What's Happening To Me?* New York: Carol Publishing Group.

PAPER DOLLS AND PAPER AIRPLANES

Metropolitan Special Committee on Child Abuse. *The Child Abuse Prevention Kit.* 1320 Yonge Street, Suite 301, Toronto, Ontario,   M4T 1X2.

Metropolitan Special Committee on Child Abuse. *My Court Case: A Court Orientation Kit for Child Witnesses.* (Available to professionals involved in the preparation of child witnesses).1320 Yonge Street, Suite 301, Toronto, Ontario, M4T 1X2..

Morgan, M. *My Feelings.* Eugene, Oregon: Migima Designs.

National Film Board Of Canada. (1992). *Good Things Can Still Happen.* (Video) P.O. Box 6100, Montreal, P.Q. H3C 3H5.

National Film Board Of Canada. *The Growing-Up Series.* (Video) P.O. Box 6100, Montreal, P.Q. H3C 3H5.

Palmer, P. (1977). *Liking Myself.* San Luis Obispo, Calif.: Impact Press.

Satullo, J.A.W., Russell, R., and Bradway, P.A. (1987). *It Happens to Boys Too.* Rape Crisis Center of Berkshire County, Inc., 18 Charles St., Pittsfield, Mass. 01201.

Varley, S., and Willis, J. (1986). *The Monster Bed.* New York: Lothrop, Lee & Shepard Books.

Watcher, O. (1983). *No More Secrets for Me.* Toronto: Little, Brown, and Company Ltd.

* Most of the books listed in the above bibliography and resource section are available from Parent Books, 201 Harbord Street, Toronto, Ontario, M5S 1H6 Phone: 416-537-8334, Fax: 416-537-9499. Bibliographies on selected topics available upon request. International orders are accepted.

About the Authors

Geraldine Crisci, M.S.W., a mental health consultant in Toronto, developed and directed the first sexual abuse prevention program for preschool children in the United States. This model demonstration project was funded by the National Center on Child Sexual Abuse and Neglect. Geraldine provides assessment and treatment services to sexually abused children and their families and to children who display sexualized behavior. She is the founding member and current acting president of the Association of Sexual Abuse Prevention.

Marilynn Lay, M.S.W., a teacher and social worker with more than 18 years' clinical experience, is a school-based social worker. She has developed and facilitated a broad range of children's groups. She provides consultation and training to educators and mental health professionals.

Liana Lowenstein,M.S.W., a child and family therapist, works in the areas of child welfare and children's mental health. She specializes in the assessment and treatment of sexually abused children and has trained other mental health professionals in dealing with childhood sexual abuse. Her article "The Use of Resolution Scrapbooks With Traumatized Children" was published in a recent issue of the *Journal of Child Welfare*.

Announcing an innovative new training opportunity for
mental health professionals who provide counseling to
sexually abused children…

PAPER DOLLS & PAPER AIRPLANES:
Therapeutic Interventions for Sexually Traumatized Children

Workshops are designed to familiarize participants with a model of
intervention for working with sexually abused children. The theoretical
framework for this approach is trauma-based. The instructors will
review 13 treatment themes and provide participants with creative
activities that can be used in individual or group therapy sessions with
abused children of all ages. Experiential exercises, slide presentations,
and activity demonstrations are a part of the workshops.

Half-day, full-day, and two-day workshops are available and can be
tailored to meet your specific training and consultation needs.

ABOUT THE INSTRUCTORS

Geraldine Crisci, M.S.W. is a mental health consultant in Toronto. She
has directed a national centre on child abuse and neglect model demonstration project on sexual abuse prevention and served as one of twenty-
four consultants to the U.S. Federal Government on recommendations
for child sexual abuse treatment and prevention. Geraldine has a private
practice at the Beaches Wellness Centre in Toronto focusing on child
sexual abuse and has developed and taught numerous training seminars
related to this topic.

Liana Lowenstein, M.S.W. is a practitioner in Toronto. She has worked
in the fields of child welfare and children's mental health. Her area of
specialty is the assessment and treatment of sexually abused children.
Liana has developed a number of therapeutic interventions for traumatized children and has provided professional consultation and training to
mental health agencies based on this work.

For further information call (416) 488-7836.

More Books for You to Enjoy

Children's Domestic Abuse Program
Help children in violent homes overcome their feelings of powerlessness, guilt, and confusion. Give children the tools they need to learn nonviolent problem-solving skills. Helpful suggestions for facilitators include pacing, modeling, language, using touch and movement to stimulate trust, and more. Each of the 15 sessions, divided by age group, includes art projects, numerous handouts, and exercises.
#1501   Binder, 200p., Age 3-12 $74.95

P.S. I Love You
Covers all the basics every parent should know: discipline, listening, anger and fighting, playing feelings, and more! From discussions and handouts to nutritious snack ideas, each of the 12 sessions is planned out for you! The **S.K.I.T.** program is specially designed for working with children, to use in conjunction with **P.S. I Love You**. Available in Spanish version too.
#1506   Paper, 104p. $34.95

S.K.I.T
Support for Kids in Transition
This companion to **P.S. I Love You** is specially designed to help you create a safe, stable atmosphere for kids in transition. The manual is divided into three age groups with each of the eight sessions planned out for you, from activities and discussion to healthy snack-time treats!
#1508   Paper, 100p., Age 4-12 $34.95

Child Support
Through Small Group Counseling
This indispensable manual offers the busy facilitator, group leader, or counselor a quick and easy reference for small group work. **Child Support** has taken 15 of the hottest topics in counseling and provides six 45-minute sessions for each topic with thoroughly tested activities for two age groups, 6-9 and 9-12.
#1511   Paper, 242p., Age 6-12 $29.95

These are just a few titles available from **KIDSRIGHTS**, the nation's comprehensive source for materials on children's rights and family issues. Order by phone, fax, or mail! Please include $5.00 for shipping and handling. VISA and MasterCard accepted. Orders under $100.00 must be prepaid. NC residents, please include 6% sales tax. Call our Program Specialists for a free catalog!

KIDSRIGHTS
10100 Park Cedar Dr. Charlotte, NC 28210 800/892-5437 or 704/541-0100 FAX 704/541-0113